DK Life Stories

Helen KELLER

DK Life Stories

Helen KELLER

by Libby Romero

Illustrated by Charlotte Ager

Senior Editor Shannon Beatty
Senior Designer Joanne Clark

Project Editor Roohi Sehgal
Editor Radhika Haswani
Additional Editorial Kritika Gupta
Art Editor Roohi Rais
Project Art Editors Yamini Panwar, Radhika Banerjee
Jacket Coordinator Francesca Young
Jacket Designer Joanne Clark
DTP Designers Sachin Gupta, Vijay Kandwal
Picture Researcher Aditya Katyal
Illustrator Charlotte Ager
Pre-Producer Nadine King
Producer Basia Ossowska
Managing Editors Laura Gilbert, Monica Saigal
Deputy Managing Art Editor Ivy Sengupta
Managing Art Editor Diane Peyton Jones
Delhi Team Head Malavika Talukder
Creative Director Helen Senior
Publishing Director Sarah Larter

Subject Consultant Sue Pilkilton
Literacy Consultant Stephanie Laird

First American Edition, 2019
Published in the United States by DK Publishing
345 Hudson Street, New York, New York 10014
Copyright © 2019 Dorling Kindersley Limited
DK, a Division of Penguin Random House LLC
19 20 21 22 23 10 9 8 7 6 5 4 3 2 1
001–308814–Jan/19

A catalog record for this book is available from the Library of Congress.
ISBN: 978-1-4654-7474-2 (Paperback)
ISBN: 978-1-4654-7544-2 (Hardcover)

DK books are available at special discounts when purchased in bulk for sales promotions,
premiums, fund-raising, or educational use. For details, contact:
DK Publishing Special Markets,
345 Hudson Street, New York, New York 10014
SpecialSales@dk.com

Printed and bound in China

A WORLD OF IDEAS:
SEE ALL THERE IS TO KNOW

www.dk.com

Dear Reader,

As you read about Helen Keller's life, you realize what an amazing person she was. You can also see how easily her life could have been very different. What if her parents had put her in an institution? What if Anne Sullivan had not become her teacher? There were a lot of "ifs" in Helen's life. Fortunately for her, most of those "ifs" seemed to work out for the best.

Not everyone is so lucky. I'm sure everybody can think of someone who could use a little help. Just imagine how much better that person's life could be if someone—maybe you—stepped in. You might make a difference. You might make a friend. You might even find that helping others helps you, too. If you don't believe me, listen to Helen, who once said, "The simplest way to be happy is to do good."

Happy reading,
Libby Romero

The life of...
Helen
KeLLeR

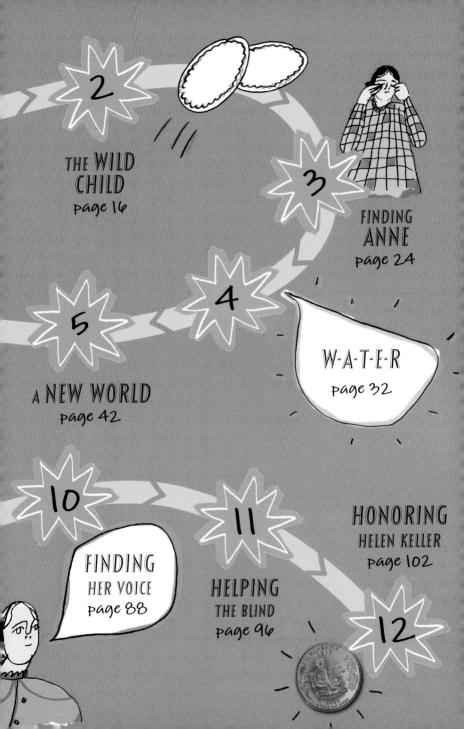

Chapter 1

Into THE darkness

Helen Keller was both blind and deaf, but she wasn't always that way. As an infant, she could see and hear everything around her.

Helen was born on June 27, 1880, in Tuscumbia, Alabama, a little town in the northwestern corner of the state. The small two-room cottage where she was born was covered with vines and climbing flowers. The cottage was part of the Keller family estate. Helen's grandfather had bought the land many years earlier. Over time, the place became known as "Ivy Green," because English ivy covered the main house and the trees and fences that were around it.

Helen's father, Arthur, was a friendly man who loved to tell stories. He was very sociable, and would often invite friends to stay for long visits at Ivy Green.

Arthur came from a family with strong southern roots, and he was even related to the American South's most famous general, Robert E. Lee. Arthur had been a captain in the Confederate Army during the Civil War as well.

Robert E. Lee

WHAT WAS THE CIVIL WAR?

The American Civil War was fought from 1861-65. The Union, representing the northern states, battled against the Confederacy, which consisted of 11 southern states that wanted to form their own country. The sides disagreed about slavery, and the war was one of the bloodiest conflicts in United States' history.

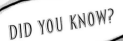
In 1877, Arthur's first wife, Sarah, died. He now had two nearly grown sons, named William and James, to raise on his own. One year later, he married Kate Adams, Helen's mother.

Kate, a young educated woman from Memphis, Tennessee, was a true southern belle. Her father had been a brigadier general in the Confederate Army, but she was related to some of the most influential families in the North. That connection shaped many of her beliefs.

Like many southerners, Arthur lost most of his money during the Civil War. To earn a living after the war, he grew cotton and became editor of the local newspaper. To help make ends meet, Kate grew her own fruits and vegetables, raised livestock, and

what is a southern belle?
A young woman from the south of the United States. A southern belle often comes from a wealthy background.

also made her own butter and lard. The family's fortunes didn't improve until 1885, when President Grover Cleveland appointed Arthur as Marshal of Alabama.

One bright spot during the years of hardship was the birth of Helen, the couple's first child. In many ways, Helen took after her mother—she had the same soft golden curls and pale blue eyes, and she had also inherited Kate's intelligence.

Helen loved to imitate others, and at just six months old, she was repeating things she'd heard people say, such as "H d'ye" and "tea, tea, tea." She also said "wah-wah," for "water."

Physically, Helen was flourishing, too. On her first birthday, Helen didn't just take her first steps—she ran. Helen would later recall how she chased "the flickering shadows of leaves that danced in the sunlight." The jaunt ended quickly, though, and Helen plunked back down to the ground. Crying, she reached out for her mother's protective arms.

Then one February day, when she was just over 18 months old, Helen got sick. For several days, she slept, plagued by a high fever. The family doctor came to examine her, and he told her family that she had "acute congestion of the stomach and brain." He didn't know if Helen would live.

Then, as suddenly as it had appeared, the fever went away. Helen's family was happy and relieved—their baby, they thought, was going to be okay.

BABIES AND COMMUNICATION

No two babies are the same. But in general, babies do develop certain skills at different stages of their lives. Some of the biggest steps in learning how to communicate are:

2 MONTHS
Coos, makes gurgling sounds.
Turns head toward sounds.

4 MONTHS
Begins to babble and copy sounds.
Cries in different ways to show hunger, pain, or being tired.

But Helen's family didn't know that her eyes hurt, and that they felt hot and dry. Her family didn't notice that Helen looked toward the wall instead of following the light, which had previously intrigued her. And even as Kate tried to comfort her baby, she didn't understand why Helen seemed so scared and confused.

That all changed a few days later when Kate waved her hand in front of Helen's face and noticed that Helen didn't close her eyes. Then the dinner bell rang.

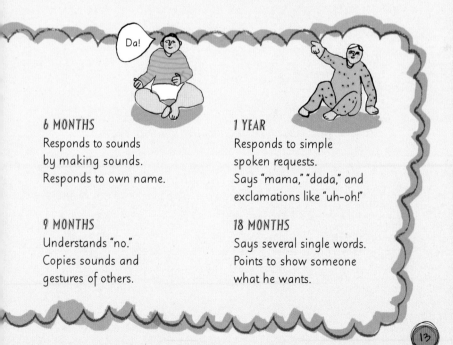

6 MONTHS
Responds to sounds by making sounds. Responds to own name.

1 YEAR
Responds to simple spoken requests. Says "mama," "dada," and exclamations like "uh-oh!"

9 MONTHS
Understands "no." Copies sounds and gestures of others.

18 MONTHS
Says several single words. Points to show someone what he wants.

It startled Kate, but Helen didn't react— and that's when Kate knew that something was wrong. Helen, her daughter who had so enjoyed the sights of beautiful flowers and the sounds of songbirds, could no longer see or hear and she'd never learned to speak more than a few words.

This was caused by her illness, which the doctor simply called "brain fever." Doctors back then didn't have the tests and tools that they have today. Looking back, however, Helen probably had either meningitis, which causes swelling of the brain, or scarlet fever.

WHAT IS SCARLET FEVER?

Scarlet fever is a disease that people sometimes get if they have strep throat. Symptoms include a bright red rash, a sore throat, and a high fever. Scarlet fever is most common in children, and it used to be a serious childhood illness. Today, doctors can treat it with antibiotics.

"The odors of fruits waft me to my southern home, to my childhood frolics in the peach orchard."

Helen Keller,
The Open Door,
1957

2

The **wild child**

The next few years were a challenge, both for Helen and everyone around her. Helen was very intelligent and also very good at getting herself into trouble!

At first, Helen relied completely on her mother for protection. When Kate sat, Helen sat in her lap, and when Kate moved, Helen clung to her skirts. As they walked around, Helen explored with her hands, and before long, she could feel her way around the house and grounds at Ivy Green.

Without the help of sight and sound, Helen relied on taste, smell, and touch to understand the world around her, and she did her best to communicate with others. If Helen shook her head, she meant "No," while a nod meant "Yes." Helen pushed when she wanted to say "Go," and she pulled to tell someone to "Come."

Helen used her early talent for imitation to communicate other ideas. For example, if she wanted bread, she acted like she was cutting and buttering slices of bread. If she wanted ice cream, she acted like she was making ice cream and shivered to show that she was cold.

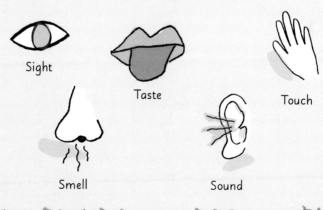

SENSING THE WORLD

There are five main senses through which animals—including people—observe the world around them. Different parts of the body can sense different things.

Sight

Taste

Touch

Smell

Sound

In this way, Helen created her own language that she used with her family and friends.

Helen's mother understood her signs, and so did Martha Washington, the young daughter of the Kellers' cook. Martha and Helen were constant playmates and, like Helen, Martha was a bit mischievous. She also knew that Helen would fight to get her way, so rather than risk getting pummeled, Martha usually gave in and did what Helen wanted.

The girls spent a lot of time in the kitchen, where they helped Martha's mother knead dough and make ice cream. They also fed the chickens that strutted up to the kitchen steps.

One day, a hen grabbed an entire tomato out of Helen's hand and ran off with it. The girls, inspired by the hen's actions, planned a heist of their own. They snatched a newly frosted cake and rushed to the woodpile to eat it!

Helen loved dogs from a very young age. Here she is as a child, with her dog.

19

Another time, the girls were on the porch cutting out paper dolls. They soon became bored with the activity, and Helen convinced Martha to let her cut her hair. Helen snipped off a big bunch of Martha's hair with the scissors, and then Martha grabbed one of Helen's long curls and cut it off in retaliation. Luckily, Helen's mother discovered them and put an end to that game.

Helen's signs helped her to express herself, but soon they were not enough. She had started to feel people's faces as they talked because she knew other people used their mouths to communicate. However, as hard as Helen tried, she could not do this.

Helen had always been a stubborn child, but now she was frustrated, too. She would later describe the feeling of not being able to communicate as "invisible hands" holding her. The only way Helen knew how to express herself was through her actions, so she kicked and hit, and threw dishes across the room.

"I felt as if invisible hands were holding me, and I made frantic efforts to free myself."

Helen Keller,
The Story of My Life,
1903

21

Helen couldn't see or hear how she was hurting others, but her behavior only got worse. Nobody had the heart to make her stop because they felt sorry for her. Pretty soon, friends and relatives were calling Helen a monster and a wild child. They told Helen's parents that it was time to send her to live in an institution, or hospital.

The Kellers had taken Helen to several doctors over the years, and all of them said there was nothing they could do. Helen's mother refused to send her away, but then a series of events convinced her that they needed to find help.

First, there was the fire. Helen had spilled water on her apron, and to dry it, she moved

closer to the fireplace. She got too close and her clothes caught on fire. A nurse wrapped Helen in a blanket and smothered the flames before she got too badly burned.

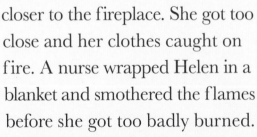

Then, when Helen discovered how to use keys, she pulled a prank on her mother. One day, Helen locked her mom in the pantry and sat on the front porch and laughed. She could feel the floor vibrating as her mother pounded on the door. It took three hours for someone to come and rescue her mother.

The final straw came when Helen became a danger to her new baby sister, Mildred. Helen was jealous of Mildred, who now seemed to be getting all of their mother's attention. One day, Helen discovered Mildred sleeping in a toy cradle, which was one of Helen's most prized possessions. Furious, Helen toppled the cradle. Luckily, Kate caught Mildred before she fell to the floor, but the Kellers needed serious help—as soon as possible.

Chapter 3

Finding Anne

Helen was now six, and she was miserable. She had tantrums every day until she was worn out. Her parents didn't know what to do to help her.

There were schools for the blind or the deaf, but none of the schools were close to the Kellers' home in Alabama. Helen was both blind *and* deaf, so finding someone willing and able to teach her seemed impossible.

Then Helen's mother read a book by Charles Dickens called *American Notes*. In that book, Dickens wrote about a woman named Laura Bridgman (1829–89).

Like Helen, Laura was both blind and deaf, but she was also educated. Laura Bridgman was the first blind and deaf person to learn language. At the age of two,

Laura got scarlet fever. When she recovered, she could no longer see, hear, or smell. She also lost most of her sense of taste.

Laura Bridgman learned language despite being blind and deaf.

Like Helen, Laura made up her own signs that she used to communicate, but her temper tantrums made her nearly impossible to manage. Just before her eighth birthday, a doctor named Samuel Gridley Howe brought Laura to the Perkins Institution for the Blind in Boston, Massachusetts. There, he taught her how to read and write.

THE PERKINS INSTITUTION FOR THE BLIND

The Perkins Institution opened in 1832. It was the first school for the blind in the United States. Perkins taught its students to explore the world with their fingertips. The school wanted its students to be educated and able to lead independent lives.

At the Perkins Institution, Laura first learned language through labels with raised letters placed on items. Later on, she learned how to fingerspell the manual alphabet in people's hands. Deaf people communicate with the manual alphabet. It uses a different hand position to show each letter of the alphabet.

Fingerspelling is a way of spelling words with hand movements into a "listener's" hand. Sometimes, people use fingerspelling if they don't know the sign for a word. They also use it to spell words for which there is no sign, like the names of people and places.

When the Kellers learned about Laura,

This is Helen with Edith Thomas, a Perkins student.

they suddenly had hope for their daughter. Helen was a smart girl—if Laura could learn to communicate, then so could Helen.

At about the same time, Helen's father heard about an eye doctor in Baltimore, Maryland. This doctor had helped some people see again after other doctors told them they would be blind forever. So in the summer of 1886, the Kellers took a train to Baltimore.

For Helen, this was a great adventure where she made friends with other passengers. One woman gave her lots of seashells to play with, and the conductor let her hang onto his coattails as he collected tickets.

When the doctor saw Helen, he said he couldn't fix her eyesight. But he did see how smart she was, and he agreed that Helen could be taught. He told the Kellers to visit Dr. Alexander Graham Bell in Washington, D.C.

Dr. Bell had taught many deaf people how to speak, so the Kellers got back on the train and went to see him. During their visit, Helen sat on Dr. Bell's knee and played with his watch. She used her signs to communicate with him, and he understood! The two became fast friends.

Dr. Bell told Helen's parents that their daughter needed a private teacher, and that they would likely find one at the Perkins Institution.

FAMOUS FRIENDS

Dr. Alexander Graham Bell (1847–1922) was a lifelong friend of Helen's. He was a scientist, inventor, and teacher of the deaf. Both his grandfather and father were speech experts, and his mother and wife were deaf. Many of Dr. Bell's inventions were machines to help the deaf. His most famous invention of all was the telephone.

That was the same school where Laura Bridgman had learned to read and write.

Helen's father wrote to the school at once, and a few weeks later, the school's director, Michael Anagnos, wrote back. He had someone who could teach Helen—her name was Anne Mansfield Sullivan.

Anne Sullivan was a recent graduate of the Perkins Institution, and she was the top student in her class. More importantly, though, she was one teacher who could truly understand what Helen was going through. This was because Anne, herself, was nearly blind.

When she was about five years old, Anne got an eye infection. Her eyes itched, so she rubbed them and the infection spread. Anne's parents had no money for a doctor, so they waited and hoped the infection would go away. It just got worse.

---

what is a graduate?

Someone who has an academic degree. A graduate will usually receive a diploma to show that they have completed schooling.

Unlike Helen, Anne had not grown up in a loving home. Anne's mother had died and her father couldn't take care of her and her younger brother, Jimmie. Her other relatives refused to help, so when Anne was 10, she and Jimmie went to live in a home called a poorhouse.

The poorhouse was called Tewksbury Almshouse, and it was a horrible, dirty place. Three months after they arrived, Jimmie died, and Anne was all alone.

Anne lived at Tewksbury for four years, and while she was there, she learned to fight for what she wanted. After she heard about Perkins—a special school for the blind—she fought for that, too. At age 14, Anne became a Perkins student.

DID YOU KNOW?

Anne was only 20 years old when she became Helen's teacher.

Anne had never been to school before, and she didn't know how to read, write, add, or subtract. So she started out in kindergarten and quickly worked her way up.

However, school was only part of Anne's education. At Perkins, she also learned manners and how to control her wild temper. She learned how to speak kindly to others, and she also had two operations on her eyes so that she could see better. At Perkins, Anne got all of the tools she needed to be ready for what would become her life's work—teaching Helen.

W-A-T-E-R

**It had been months since Anne had agreed to
teach Helen. Anne used that time to read all of
Dr. Howe's notes on teaching Laura Bridgman.**

On March 3, 1887, Anne finally arrived in
Tuscumbia, Alabama—Helen's hometown.
Helen's mother and her stepson James went to
meet her at the train station. They told Anne
that they had been coming to the station for
the past two days because they weren't sure
when she was going to arrive.

Helen was waiting back on the front porch at their home, Ivy Green. For the past few days, she had noticed that her mother was hurrying around, and she knew someone important was coming to visit. In fact, Helen would later write that "the most important day" in her life was when her teacher, Anne Sullivan, arrived.

Helen liked visitors because they usually brought her something delicious to eat. So when Helen felt footsteps on the porch, she rushed forward to greet the visitor, and her hands flew into action. She felt Anne's face and dress, and then she felt Anne's bag. It would not open, so Helen found the keyhole and made her sign for turning a key—she was determined to get to any treats hidden inside.

"The most **important day** I remember in all my life is the one on which **my teacher,** Anne Mansfield Sullivan, **came to me.**"

Helen Keller,
The Story of My Life,
1903

Helen's mother told her to stop, so Helen had a temper tantrum. However, the tantrum ended quickly after Anne let Helen hold her watch. Then she and Helen went upstairs to Anne's room to begin their work together.

Anne studied Helen as the two of them unpacked her luggage. Helen was not the pale, delicate child she had expected. She was big and strong and full of energy. Anne could see that Helen was smart, but something was missing. Helen hardly ever smiled.

Helen was on a mission, and when she found a doll in Anne's trunk, she started to play with it. The doll was a gift from the blind children at the Perkins Institution. Laura Bridgman, who still lived at Perkins, had dressed it herself!

To Anne, this seemed like the perfect time to start teaching Helen. She spelled "d-o-l-l" in Helen's hand and then pointed

Anne used a doll like this one to teach Helen.

to the doll and nodded her head. Anne had noticed that Helen always nodded her head to show that something belonged to her.

It took several attempts, but soon Helen copied the motions. Helen did not understand that "d-o-l-l" spelled a word that meant "doll," but she did figure out that if she copied the motions she got to keep the doll.

For the next few days, Anne tried to teach, and Helen had a tantrum every time she failed to get her way. This behavior worked with Helen's family, but Anne needed it to stop. One day during breakfast, Anne took action.

HELEN'S DOLLS

Helen had lots of dolls when she was young. Sometimes, she treated them like they were her babies, but usually she wasn't very careful with them. She soaked one doll when she tried to feed it milk, and she planted another doll in the garden so it would grow. During one of her tantrums, she even smashed the porcelain doll Anne gave her.

Helen had bad table manners. She touched other people's plates and grabbed whatever she wanted to eat. That morning, Anne wouldn't let Helen touch her plate. Helen tried again and again. Anne refused, so Helen lay down on floor and had a tantrum. Her family was so upset by the scene that Anne asked them to leave.

Eventually, Helen stopped kicking and screaming. She stood up and walked around the table. Anne was the only other person in the room. Anne was still eating, and she wouldn't let Helen take her food. After about two hours—and fights over using a napkin and a spoon—Helen gave in and finished her own breakfast.

Anne knew that she would not be able to teach Helen until the girl learned how to obey her. She also knew that would not happen if Helen's family was around, since they gave in to her whims every time Helen had a tantrum.

So Anne talked with Helen's parents, and they agreed to let her live alone with Helen. The two of them would move into the cottage where Helen was born. Helen's family would still be nearby, but they would stay away and give Anne the space she needed to teach Helen.

Helen and Anne lived in the cottage for the next two weeks and, at first, Helen fought against everything. She even knocked out one of Anne's teeth! Soon, however, Helen seemed to understand what was happening. She and Anne were all alone, and Anne was in charge.

Helen played with her dolls, and she learned how to sew and string beads. She also learned a few new words, and she and Anne spent a lot of time exploring the gardens around the cottage.

Here's Helen a few years later in 1892, with her teacher, Anne Sullivan.

Helen would later read special books using her fingertips.

Helen's family could see them, but stayed out of their way. They were surprised at the progress Anne was making with their little girl. Helen was changing—she was quiet, and she was starting to behave for Anne.

Soon after Helen and Anne moved back into the main house, Helen could spell 21 words—but she still didn't understand that everything had a name. She didn't know that her fingers were spelling those names.

Two words that Helen kept mixing up were "m-u-g" and "m-i-l-k." She acted like she was drinking when she spelled either one. Then one day, Helen wanted to know the name for "water," and this gave Anne an idea.

She took Helen to the water pump. Anne had Helen hold her mug under the pump as cold water came pouring out. At the same time, she spelled "w-a-t-e-r" in Helen's other hand.

Suddenly, Helen understood that the wonderful, wet, cool thing flowing over her hand was "w-a-t-e-r." Helen spelled the word in her hand several times. She dropped her mug and pointed to other things for Anne to name. She learned to spell "d-i-r-t" and "p-u-m-p." She pointed to Anne and asked her name, and Anne taught her to spell the word "t-e-a-c-h-e-r." By the end of the day, Helen had learned to spell and understand 30 new words.

This is what the water pump at the Kellers' home looked like.

---

what is a water pump?

A device that pulls up water from a well. When you push the handle of a water pump, it draws water up and out of a spout.

A new world

Now that Helen knew what words were, she was eager to learn the name of everything she touched. Anne would spell them out in her hand.

Most children Helen's age were educated in classrooms, but Anne knew that Helen wasn't ready for that just yet. Helen couldn't learn lessons if she didn't have the vocabulary to understand them—but what was the best way to teach her the words she needed to know?

Anne found the answer after watching Helen's cousin, who was a baby. Babies, she thought, understood what words meant long before they spoke. That's because they listened to what was going on around them, and when they finally spoke, they imitated the sounds they had heard. If that's how babies learned language, Helen could do the same.

From that point on, Anne didn't just spell single words in Helen's hand, but complete sentences. She spelled out entire conversations for the young girl, with the hope that one day, Helen would know what to imitate.

Helen was behaving better now, but she was still full of energy. Anne knew that she would never get Helen to sit quietly in a classroom, but that wasn't how she wanted to teach anyway. She wanted Helen to learn through exploring her world.

UNDERSTANDING IDEAS

Early on, Helen could only learn the names of things she could touch. Then one day she was trying to make a pattern with beads, but she kept making mistakes. Anne tapped her head and spelled "t-h-i-n-k." Suddenly, Helen understood that she was thinking in her head! Some things—like thinking and love—couldn't be touched. They were ideas, but they had names, too.

The world became their classroom, and if they were indoors, they would play games. One of their favorite activities was a type of hide-and-seek, where Anne would hide specific objects, and Helen would have to find them.

Outside, they took long walks and, as they walked, Helen learned about nature and the world around her. She held crickets and felt the movement of their legs when they chirped. She held an egg just as it hatched to reveal a baby chick, and she touched new plants and discovered how they grew up from the ground.

One of their favorite walks took them to Keller's Landing. This old dock on the Tennessee River was about two miles (3.2 km) from Ivy Green. For Helen and Anne, Keller's Landing was the perfect place to play in the mud. They built dams out of rocks, dug out lakes and rivers, and formed huge mountains out of mud. Helen thought this was fun, but what she didn't realize was that it was a lesson—Anne was teaching her geography.

Anne was ready to teach Helen how to read, but first, she had to familiarize Helen with the letters of the alphabet. Anne wrote words Helen already knew in raised letters on paper cards. Then she put the words on top of the objects they named— she placed "b-o-x," for example, on top of a box.

Initially, Helen didn't understand, so Anne made the lesson simpler. She put Helen's hand on a new card. Anne spelled the shape on Helen's other hand—it was the letter A! Helen understood! By the end of the day, she knew the entire alphabet.

Next came words. Anne had a book that was written in raised letters. She placed Helen's finger on the word "c-a-t," and then she spelled "c-a-t" into Helen's other hand. Helen was thrilled because she knew the word! Soon, Helen and Anne had a new game, which involved who could find words from the book the quickest.

Once Helen understood words, Anne taught her how to sort them into sentences. Then she showed Helen how to write using a grooved writing board.

Helen loved learning, and she loved language in particular. She constantly asked questions and begged Anne to tell her stories. Anne spelled as long and as fast as she could, but sometimes she became too tired to go on. That didn't stop Helen, though. Helen spelled in her baby sister's hand and she spelled in her dog's paw. She even carried on lively conversations with herself, spelling in her own hand!

what is a grooved writing board?

A special board placed between sheets of paper. The grooves are like lines, and they help blind writers keep their words even.

Helen never stopped, and when she became thin and pale, her parents began to worry. In order to keep Helen busy and her parents happy, Anne had Helen do less active lessons.

Helen wrote for hours, and soon her pencil writing was excellent. Anne started to teach Helen how to use braille, which is a system that allows people to read with their fingertips. With braille, Helen could write words that she could feel and read to herself.

WHAT IS BRAILLE?

Braille is a code that lets people read with their fingers. It was invented by Louis Braille, a blind French teenager, in 1825. There is a character for each letter, number, and punctuation mark. Each one is made up of a different combination of six raised dots. The dots are arranged in a cell with two columns and three rows—just like a domino.

Helen also spent a lot of time counting. First, she counted everything in the house, and then she counted all the words in her book. Helen liked counting so much that Anne joked she might even start counting the hairs on her head! Helen was eager to learn about the new and exciting world all around her!

There were many places to explore at Ivy Green, but for Helen to learn even more, she needed to explore other places as well. So when the circus came to town, the whole family went along. Helen loved the circus! She got to feed elephants and pet baby lions, and she even got to shake hands with a trained black bear! She played with monkeys and felt a giraffe's long neck. She met the circus performers, too. They let her touch their costumes and feel how they moved as they performed their routines. There was so much Helen wanted to learn!

At Christmastime, Helen went to town to celebrate at the local school. She taught several girls how to spell with their fingers and quickly made friends. For the first time in her young life, Helen understood what the Christmas holiday was, and she could share the experience with her family and friends. Helen's parents thanked Anne for making this possible. Helen was finally engaging with the world around her, and her world was about to become much bigger.

The miracle child

In May 1888, seven-year-old Helen, Anne, and Mrs. Keller took a train to Boston. They were on their way to visit the Perkins Institution.

Helen was excited about their trip. On the way, they stopped in Washington, D.C., to visit Helen's friend Alexander Graham Bell. They also went to the White House and met President Grover Cleveland.

Mr. Michael Anagnos, the director of the Perkins Institution, had invited them to visit the school, and from the moment they arrived, Helen and Anne were treated like celebrities.

Helen had written letters to the Perkins

students, and she and Anne had written to Mr. Anagnos, too. Anne had even written reports describing how she taught and what Helen had learned.

Helen and Mr. Anagnos

Mr. Anagnos was delighted with Helen's progress, and he wrote about it in the school's newsletter. However, in his excitement, Mr. Anagnos exaggerated the facts, and when the newspapers outside the school wrote about Helen, they would embellish her story even further. Helen and Anne were already famous at this point, but many of the things that were being written about them were simply not true.

---

what does embellish mean?

To add extra details that may not be true in order to make something sound better. People sometimes embellish a story.

Helen and Anne visited friends on their summer vacation in Cape Cod.

Helen didn't know the stories people told about her at Perkins, but Anne did, and she was not happy with them. She thought the truth was impressive enough.

As guests at Perkins, Anne and Helen could read the raised-print and braille books in the school's library. They could explore

the impressive collection of stuffed animals, seashells, flowers, and plants, and they could also visit nearby places like

Bunker Hill and Plymouth Rock to learn about the local history.

For Helen, the best part was meeting the students she had been writing to for nearly a year. For the first

time in her life, she could talk to children her age in her own language. All of the

students at Perkins were blind, so they knew

the manual alphabet. Like Helen, they talked with their hands.

When Perkins closed for the summer, Helen, her mother, and Anne went to visit a friend in Cape Cod, Massachusetts. While there, Helen got her first taste of the ocean— literally! Full of excitement, she ran straight into the water, but her elation, or joy, only lasted until a wave swept over her head. Then fear took over, as Helen made her way back to Anne on the beach. Shaking, she demanded to know, "Who put salt in the water?"

The next winter, Helen
and Anne returned to Perkins.
One of the teachers had just
returned from Norway, and
she told Helen about a deaf
and blind Norwegian girl
who had learned to speak.
Helen wanted to do the same.

Sarah Fuller

Anne didn't know how to
teach a blind and deaf person to speak, so
she searched for the best teacher she could
find. Soon, Helen began to take lessons with
Sarah Fuller, the principal of the Horace Mann
School for the Deaf in Boston.

As with many other things, Helen
learned to speak through
touch. When Miss Fuller
made sounds, she put Helen's
hand on her face, and she let
Helen feel her lips, tongue, and
throat. Helen imitated what she
had felt, and in just 11 lessons,

she had learned all of the basic sounds. In less than a month, Helen spoke her first sentence. She said, "It is warm."

Helen's speech was not perfect. Most people could not understand what she said, but she and Anne worked hard to make it better.

With Anne's help, Helen worked hard on her speech, but Helen was never happy with her spoken voice. Many people found it hard to understand.

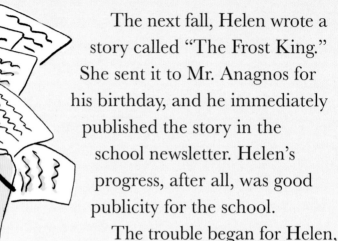

The next fall, Helen wrote a story called "The Frost King." She sent it to Mr. Anagnos for his birthday, and he immediately published the story in the school newsletter. Helen's progress, after all, was good publicity for the school.

The trouble began for Helen, though, when someone wrote to the school. They said that 11-year-old Helen had copied another story called "The Frost Fairies," by Margaret T. Canby.

Helen had never heard of "The Frost Fairies," and neither had Anne, but the two stories were very much alike. After a bit of investigating, Anne discovered that someone else had read the story to Helen several years ago, and Helen had accidentally written it from memory.

Unfortunately, many people thought Helen had copied "The Frost Fairies" on purpose, including her former champion, Mr. Anagnos. At first, Mr. Anagnos said he believed Helen when she told him what had happened. Then he changed his mind and accused her of plagiarism. He also said that Anne should no longer be allowed to teach Helen.

DID YOU KNOW?

Helen and Anne loved to go tobogganing, or sledding, during Boston's snowy winters.

School leaders questioned Helen for two hours. Four of them thought she was guilty, four thought she was innocent, and, eventually, Mr. Anagnos broke the tie and voted in Helen's favor. Despite his change of heart, Helen and Anne felt betrayed.

Helen's friend, author Mark Twain, called the people who accused her of plagiarism "a collection of decayed human turnips."

what does plagiarism mean? Using someone else's words and claiming that they are your own.

In the spring of 1893, Helen and Anne left Perkins and returned to Helen's home at Ivy Green. Helen needed some time to emotionally recover from the shame and betrayal she had experienced at Perkins.

She was upset, and for a while, she even stopped talking and reading. Helen was also afraid to write because she didn't know which thoughts were her own and which were memories of what others had said.

The cover of *The Youth's Companion*, World's Columbian Exposition at Chicago Issue, 1893.

After the "The Frost King" disaster, Helen struggled with her self-confidence, but then a children's magazine called *The Youth's Companion* contacted her. They asked Helen to write

IMPACTFUL LETTERS

When Helen was at Perkins, her dog died. Friends were raising money to buy her a new one, but Helen wrote letters to them, asking that they send the money to Tommy Stringer instead. Tommy was a five-year-old blind and deaf boy. He lived in a poorhouse and there was no money to get him a teacher. Helen was just a child, but people listened to her letters. Helen's friends and supporters sent enough money to send Tommy to Perkins.

about her life. Anne thought it was a good idea, and she encouraged Helen to do it. Although Helen never wrote fiction again, she did write about her life.

Around this time, Helen also learned that her letters could make a difference in other people's lives. She slowly got her confidence back, and she began writing letters and poems to family and friends again.

Chapter 7

A **star** student

Now that Helen was on the mend, it was time for her and Anne to continue their pursuit of adventure and academic studies.

Dr. Bell had become one of Helen's best friends and biggest supporters. As a surprise for Anne, he and Helen planned a trip to Niagara Falls. As soon as they got there, Helen could feel the power of Niagara's water—even in their hotel, it made the glass in the windows shake! Helen was thrilled with the water's astonishing force. It was the same feeling she'd had the first time she went to the ocean.

That summer, Helen and Anne visited Chicago, Illinois. Dr. Bell had invited them to join him at the World's Fair, an exhibition that showcases the achievements of different countries. Helen was allowed to touch the exhibits, so for the next three weeks, she explored everything with her fingertips. Helen felt Viking ships and bronze statues, and she searched for diamonds. She learned about, but refused to touch, mummies. Helen also explored new inventions, such as the telephone. Dr. Bell explained how the devices worked.

Anne and Helen with friends on their trip to Niagara Falls in 1893.

After the World's Fair, Helen and Anne returned to Ivy Green, where they got back to work on Helen's education. Helen studied arithmetic, literature, French, and Latin, and she also practiced speaking. However, no matter how hard Helen tried, she knew she didn't sound like everyone else—and if there was one thing Helen wanted, that was it.

When Helen was 14, it seemed like her dream might actually come true. The leaders of the Wright-Humason School for the Deaf in New York City said they could help her speak like everyone else.

John Spaulding, one of Helen's wealthy supporters, offered to pay her expenses.

So in the fall of 1894, Helen and Anne moved to New York City. Helen and Anne loved exploring their new city. They walked through Central Park, sailed on the Hudson River, and visited the Statue of Liberty. At her new school, Helen studied math, geography, and French. She learned how to speak German and read lips.

Lip reading was a challenge. Most deaf

Helen and Anne visited the Statue of Liberty.

WHAT IS LIP READING?

Lip reading is a way to "read" or understand spoken words without hearing them. When people lip read, they watch the speaker's mouth, and they also study the speaker's facial expressions and body movements. Because Helen couldn't see these things, she had to feel them with her hands.

people learn how to read lips by watching other people speak, but Helen couldn't do that because she couldn't see. So Helen learned by touch, just like she did when she first learned to speak. Helen struggled when people spoke quickly, but she soon learned how to read lips.

Helen also worked hard to make her voice easier to understand, but she wasn't as successful with this endeavor. The goal was to improve her voice—not just how she said words, but the way her voice sounded. She even took singing lessons, but they didn't work. No matter how hard Helen tried, it was still hard for other people to understand what she said.

63

During Helen's second year at the Wright-Humason School, both her father and Mr. Spaulding died. Helen had recently become very religious and took comfort in her beliefs. She also kept busy preparing for her next goal—Helen wanted to go to college.

Helen, however, wasn't ready for college yet because she still had a lot to learn. She couldn't get what she needed at the Wright-Humason School, so it was time to go somewhere else.

Anne found the perfect place—the Cambridge School for Young Ladies. Many girls went there to prepare for Radcliffe College, but none of those girls were blind and deaf.

Helen had to get special permission to attend, and she also needed money to cover the costs. Luckily, her friends came to the rescue, and created a fund to pay her expenses.

Learning at the Cambridge School was challenging. None of the teachers could fingerspell, and the school didn't have any books written in raised print or braille.

It was up to Anne to relay everything to Helen. Helen had to remember it all and type it up later.

Eventually, Helen's supporters sent a few braille books, and Arthur Gilman, the school's principal, learned how to fingerspell. Helen's German teacher learned to fingerspell, too. Best of all, Helen's mother and little sister, Mildred, came to visit at Christmas. Mr. Gilman even invited Mildred to stay and study at the school.

HELEN'S COLLEGE DREAM

College was not a new dream for Helen. As a young girl she announced that she wanted to go to Harvard, but that was impossible. At the time, Harvard was only a college for men. So Helen set her sights on Radcliffe College, which was Harvard's partner school for female students.

The year flew by and Helen passed all of her classes, two of them with honors.

Since Helen's first year had been such a success, Mr. Gilman decided she would be ready for Radcliffe in just three more years. Helen's

Arthur Gilman

second year at Cambridge, however, did not go as well as her first.

Unfortunately for Helen, Mr. Gilman wanted her to study more math. Helen hated the subject. Now she would have to take even more advanced math classes and, to pass, she would need the help of an excellent tutor.

To complicate matters, many of the supplies Helen had ordered hadn't arrived. One of those items was a new braillewriter—a sort of typewriter that printed raised letters in braille. Helen needed this for her classes.

In addition, Helen's classes were bigger than ever before. Her teachers no longer had time to give her special instruction, so everything fell to Anne. Anne's eyesight was getting worse, and, for the first time, Helen worried that Anne wouldn't be able to keep up.

Just as things started to get better, Helen got sick. Mr. Gilman blamed Anne, and he wrote to Helen's mother and said Anne was pushing Helen too hard. He said she should fire Anne and put him in charge of Helen's education. Mrs. Keller was worried about her daughter, so she agreed.

Helen and Mildred were
devastated when Anne left.
So was Anne, but she wasn't
about to give up. That night,
Anne sent telegrams to Mrs.
Keller, Dr. Bell, and Joseph E.
Chamberlin, who was the
editor of *The Youth's Companion*.

The next day, Anne returned to the
school. Then Mr. Chamberlin arrived, and he
invited Anne and the Keller girls to stay with
him. When Mrs. Keller arrived at Cambridge
and saw how unhappy her daughters were, she
removed the girls from the school. After that,
Helen and Anne stayed with the Chamberlins.

Once there, Helen worked one-on-one with
her tutors, and she learned quickly.
At the end of June 1899, Helen
was finally ready to take her
college entrance exams.

Radcliffe, however, wouldn't
let Anne spell the questions
in Helen's hand. The college

wanted to make sure that Helen was doing the work herself, so the exams were copied into braille so that Helen could read them herself.

There were three different dot reading systems at the time, and Helen knew all of them. For math, however, each one used different signs and symbols. Helen was unfamiliar with the symbols they used on the test, and had only two days to learn them!

Because of this, the tests were harder for Helen than they should have been, but Helen passed them anyway. Her dream had come true—Helen was going to go to college.

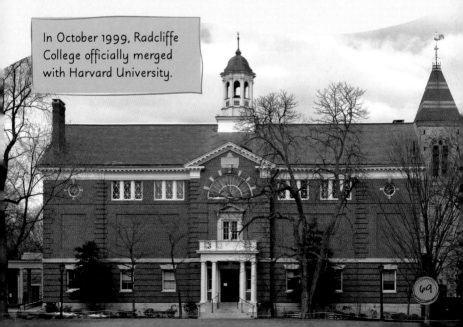

In October 1999, Radcliffe College officially merged with Harvard University.

✴ **8**

Author AND graduate

Helen had tackled many obstacles, but now she faced another challenge. The dean of Radcliffe wanted her to wait a year before starting classes.

Helen did not want to wait another year. She had even been accepted to two other prestigious, or well-respected, colleges—Cornell University and the University of Chicago. She turned them both down, however, because even though she had other options, she wanted to go to Radcliffe. So Helen agreed to the dean's demands.

For the next year, Helen studied with a private tutor. Then, Radcliffe finally agreed to let her start taking classes, but there was one condition—Helen had to take her tests alone.

What is
a dean?

Head of a college or university. A dean can also be the head of a college department.

This was due to a misconception, or false belief, that Anne might have been the true genius in their partnership. Because of this, Anne could fingerspell for Helen in class, but she could not be there when Helen took tests.

Instead, Helen would have to take her tests in a room all alone, where a teacher would type the tests in braille, and Helen would answer in braille. The head of the college would be there to supervise.

At the time, many people didn't believe that a blind and deaf girl like Helen could succeed in school, and others thought she shouldn't go to college because she was a woman. Back then, many people thought women were fragile, and that their minds and bodies would be damaged by higher education. Fortunately, we know better than that today.

Helen had dreamed about going to Radcliffe for years, but college was not what she had expected. Helen thought that the professors would share greatness and wisdom, but they simply taught lessons. What's more is that they taught so quickly that Helen had trouble keeping up, and there was so much work that Helen had no time left to just sit and think. To make matters worse, all of the reading made Anne's eyesight weaker than ever.

College was lonely for Helen, too. She was different and she was also famous, so she didn't fit in. The other girls tried to be nice—they even got her a dog. However, without Anne's help, Helen could only communicate directly with two students. One girl knew how to fingerspell, and another had learned braille, but because she could communicate with so few fellow students, it was hard for Helen to make friends.

DID YOU KNOW?

Helen loved dogs. In 1938, she owned the first Akita in the US.

The students at Radcliffe gave Helen a dog, which she named Phiz.

It wasn't much better with the teachers. Only one professor learned how to fingerspell, but most of the other teachers and school leaders ignored Helen and Anne.

One professor who didn't ignore Helen was Charles Copeland. Helen took Professor Copeland's English class in her sophomore year at Radcliffe. She thought his lectures were interesting and witty, and he thought her writing was excellent. Professor Copeland even said that Helen was one of the best students he had ever had.

Charles Copeland

One day, Professor Copeland told the editor of the *Ladies' Home Journal* about Helen's writing. The editor then offered Helen $3,000 to write six articles about her life.

What is a sophomore?

A second-year college student. Sophomore can also mean the second year of college.

Helen and Anne were already busy with classes, but that was too much money to turn down, so Helen agreed to write the articles.

However, it didn't take long for Helen to realize that she needed help. Adding monthly deadlines to her classwork was too much for her to handle alone. Helen needed someone to edit her work, and she found the perfect

Ladies Home Journal.
Cover of the American
magazine for July 1902.

person in John Macy. He helped Helen turn her essays from Professor Copeland's class into articles and, later, a book.

John Macy was an English instructor at Harvard University, and he had the time, intelligence, and skills to help Helen craft her articles. He even learned how to fingerspell so he could talk with Helen directly himself.

Helen in her cap and gown, which is what people wear on their graduation day.

With John's help, Helen finished her articles, and when he suggested that she expand the articles into a book, she agreed. He even found her a publisher.

Helen's book, called *The Story of My Life*, was published in 1903 during Helen's junior, or third, year at Radcliffe. Sales for *The Story of My Life* started out slowly, but it became an international bestseller.

One year later, Helen graduated from Radcliffe. It was also her 24th birthday, and with Anne by her side, she proudly accepted her diploma. She had earned a bachelor of arts degree and graduated from college with honors.

9

Helen's opinions

Helen had her diploma, but now she faced the same question all other new college graduates must answer: *What do I do next?*

For Helen, that question was complicated. She was blind and deaf, and she was also a woman. Because of prejudiced attitudes toward people like Helen, her job options were limited.

Helen's supporters had paid most of her expenses up until now, but she wanted to make her own money so she could support herself. Since *The Story of My Life* had become an international bestseller, Helen and Anne were more famous than ever.

After her first book's success, Helen decided to become a professional author. Not only would that help pay the bills, it would also keep her in the spotlight. That was important because Helen really wanted to make a difference. She wanted to help other blind and deaf people, just as people had helped her.

Helping other people was nothing new for Helen. As a child, she had written letters asking her supporters to send money to educate other blind and deaf children. While at Radcliffe, she had spoken to legislators in New York and Massachusetts, asking them to fund more job training programs for blind people.

Helen had also written an article called "I Must Speak" for the *Ladies' Home Journal.* In the article, she told readers about an eye infection that mothers can pass on to their babies. The cure was simple—babies just needed special eye drops.

The eye drops didn't cost much, but not all parents could afford them. Tragically, babies who had this infection and didn't get the eye drops would lose their eyesight.

Helen had always believed there was no way to prevent blindness, but now she knew that this was not the case. Knowing that so much blindness could have been prevented made her angry.

Helen saw the connection between blindness and poverty. She wanted to learn more about the struggles poor people faced, so she visited their neighborhoods. She talked with workers and immigrants to learn about their lives. She wanted to know how she could help because Helen felt it was important to improve the lives of others.

HELEN AND THE ACLU

Helen didn't just talk and write about the causes she believed in—she took action. In 1920, Helen and nine other people founded the American Civil Liberties Union (ACLU), an organization devoted to protecting the freedoms and rights of all workers. The organization is still active today with more than 500,000 members in all 50 states.

"We are never really **happy** until we try to **brighten** the lives of others."

Helen Keller, undated

Throughout her life, Helen had learned from many different people, and one person who had made a big impact on her beliefs at this time was John Macy. Helen had come to admire John when he edited her book. In addition, Anne had fallen in love with him, and when John and Anne got married in 1905, Helen lived with them.

Helen

Helen with John and Anne, 1900.

Like many Americans at the time, John was a socialist, which means he didn't think that rich business owners should control all of the country's wealth. He thought that everyone should have an equal share.

John and his friends would often get together, share popcorn and cider, and talk about their political beliefs. Helen and Anne joined them as well. Helen loved the lively discussions and she agreed with what they said. John gave Helen many books to read so she could learn more about socialism, and in 1909, Helen joined the Socialist Party, too.

This was a good time for the three friends. With John's help, Helen published two more books. Anne and John were happily married, and Helen loved living with them. John often took Helen for rides on a bike built for two people—Helen loved it when they went really fast!

Best of all, Helen and Anne's relationship was changing. Instead of simply being teacher and student, Helen and Anne were becoming friends.

But there was one problem—money. Helen was working, but she wasn't earning enough money to support herself and pay Anne's salary. She still needed the help of her wealthy friends, and that, unfortunately, went against her socialist beliefs.

As a socialist, Helen wanted to help workers, for whom she believed in equality, fair wages, and good working conditions. She felt especially bad for women and children, since they often had the worst jobs and had little or no power to change anything.

Many of Helen's supporters were capitalists who owned the businesses where these people worked. So in the beginning, Helen kept quiet about her beliefs, but she and Anne were running out of money.

Andrew Carnegie was one of the wealthiest people in the world. He had sold his business and wanted to share his wealth with others. In 1910, he offered to give Helen an annual allowance, and although Helen needed the money, she kindly refused.

Andrew Carnegie

Instead, Helen wrote another book called *Out of the Dark,* in which she wrote about her socialist beliefs. The book did not sell a lot of copies. People didn't care about Helen's politics—they wanted to know more about her life.

Things were not going well for Helen and Anne. Anne and John's marriage was falling apart, and John had left. Helen had given up hope of supporting herself as an author, and money was tighter than ever. The solution, she convinced Anne, was to go on a lecture tour together.

Their first lecture took place in February 1913, but what they hadn't counted on was Helen's stage fright. When it was Helen's turn to speak onstage, she froze, and only managed to whisper. When Helen was finally done, she ran from the stage and burst into tears.

Even though it was difficult, Helen worked on her stage fright, and the two women continued on their tour. A few months later, however, Anne got sick and because they were stuck in a hotel, there was nothing Helen could do to help her. When Anne recovered, they went home.

Helen felt helpless to change her financial situation, so she wrote a letter to Andrew Carnegie. The two had become good friends over the past three years. She asked if his offer of an allowance was still good—luckily for her, it was. Despite her socialist beliefs, this time Helen accepted.

Anne and Helen during their lecture tour of the Northeastern United States in 1913.

Anne and Helen in New York at the International Flower Show in 1913.

10

Finding her voice

For the next several years, Helen and Anne traveled almost constantly. They went around the country giving their lectures.

They didn't go on their lecture tour alone this time. Helen's mother often went with them, and if she didn't, Polly Thomson went along instead. Polly was a Scottish immigrant that they had hired to help Anne with all of her duties. Anne was struggling with her workload, and she was also very sad because she and John had now separated permanently.

Helen felt strange being in the spotlight, but she had a lot

Polly Thomson

to talk about. In addition to being a socialist, she was now a suffragist as well. This means that she supported women's rights. Helen was also a pacifist, which means she was against war.

The United States was getting ready to enter World War I (1914–18). Helen thought this conflict was just a way for capitalists to make more money, so she encouraged working class people to fight against the war.

Helen's lectures were a huge success, and she sometimes spoke before crowds of more than 2,000 cheering people. However, in the summer of 1916, they came to a halt. Anne was sick and went away to recover, and Polly was in Scotland visiting her family. Helen went to stay with her mother in Alabama, and while she was there, she fell in love.

Helen, who was now 36 years old, never thought she would marry, but Peter Fagan swept her off her feet. Peter, age 29, was a socialist and a newspaperman. Helen had hired him as a temporary secretary.

The couple planned a secret wedding—they even took out a marriage license. However, their plans were ruined after Helen's mother read about the marriage license in the newspaper.

Helen's entire family was against the marriage, and so was Anne. None of them thought Helen should marry and have children. They made Peter leave, and the pair never met again.

Sadly, this was not the only part of her life that was falling apart. The US had entered World War I, and Helen's socialist and pacifist ideas were no longer popular. Some people even thought her ideas were dangerous and, because of this, fewer people wanted to hear Helen speak.

WHY COULDN'T HELEN GET MARRIED?

In the early 1900s, it was against the law in many parts of the United States for women with disabilities to get married and have children. Helen's family and friends didn't think she should get married, even though they knew this made Helen unhappy. Today, laws like this are illegal because they discriminate against people with disabilities.

Anne returned home after she recovered from her illness, and after going over their finances, she had bad news—they could no longer afford to keep their home. Helen, Anne, and Polly would have to move, and they also needed a new source of income. Fortunately, Helen's luck was about to change.

In early 1918, a Hollywood producer contacted Helen because he wanted to make a movie about her life. He promised to pay Helen $10,000 when filming began, and he said that she could earn up to $100,000 if the film was a success. The offer seemed too good to pass up.

Helen was excited about this new idea. A movie would allow her to communicate with more people than ever before. More importantly, though, it would give her the money she needed to take care of Anne.

The movie, called *Deliverance*, almost didn't get made. Just before filming began, Helen gave a speech supporting a union and its radical ideas. The film's producer panicked—he was afraid that the government would harass them if Helen kept giving speeches like that. In addition, he was worried that theaters would refuse to show their film. Helen agreed to stop giving speeches, and then she, Anne, and Polly went to Hollywood to make the movie.

Helen enjoyed making the film, but she wasn't entirely happy with the final product. She wanted the movie to be factual, but the producer wanted to create suspense. Critics gave the movie good reviews, but few people went to see it. Beyond the initial $10,000 she got when filming began, Helen didn't receive any more money for making

While in Hollywood, Polly, Helen, and Anne met many famous stars. Charlie Chaplin, standing, even invited them out to dinner.

the movie. However, Helen's career in entertainment was far from over.

Bitten by the acting bug, Helen decided to tell her story in a new way. She created a vaudeville act based on the lectures she and Anne had given years earlier. At the time, vaudeville was even more popular than films. Its acts included singers, dancers, animals, and

---

what is vaudeville?   A type of theater show popular in the US in the 1920s.

acrobats. Helen's friends tried to talk her out of her idea, but she insisted—she and Anne needed the money.

Helen and Anne's act premiered on February 24, 1920, at the Palace Theatre in New York City. They were paid $2,000 a week, and at the time, they were some of the highest-paid vaudeville performers in the world.

Helen loved the excitement of the live act, but Anne did not. Anne hated rushing around. She hated the noise, and the stage lights hurt her eyes. Plus, she kept getting sick, but she stuck with it for the money.

In November 1921, Helen and Anne were about to give a performance in Los Angeles, California. Helen received word that her mother had passed away, so she and Anne went home. When they arrived, Helen learned that her dear friend Alexander Graham Bell had died, too.

Helen and Anne were exhausted, and Anne's health was worse than ever. These challenges proved to be too much, and they never returned to vaudeville.

Helen and Anne in costume for one of their famous vaudeville performances.

11

Helping THE blind

A new opportunity came in 1924. Helen and Anne were asked to become fundraisers for the American Foundation for the Blind (AFB).

The AFB was quite a new organization, but it had already developed a single braille code for the nation. It had created a braille printing press so more books for the blind could be published, and its members also helped blind people find jobs.

Teaming up with the AFB was good for everyone. Helen could focus on a cause that was dear to her heart—helping the blind—and she and Anne would receive a regular income. The AFB, in turn, would get two powerful names to bring attention to its cause.

DID YOU KNOW?

The head of the AFB called Helen, Anne, and Polly "the Three Musketeers."

It quickly became clear just how much influence Helen's name had. She and Anne raised $21,000 at their very first fundraiser. After talking with President Calvin Coolidge, he agreed to serve as the AFB's honorary chairman.

President Calvin Coolidge

Helen held fundraisers in her home, and she spoke in churches and town halls. She and Anne worked hard to teach people about blindness, but after three years, it was time to take a break.

Helen's influential name attracted wealthy donors like Henry Ford, who gave money to the AFB.

Helen wanted to write more books, so she hired an editor named Nella Braddy Henney to help her. The first book, *My Religion*, was published in 1927. The second, *Midstream: My Later Life*, came out in 1929, but it wasn't as popular as Helen had hoped. People wanted to read about her childhood—they didn't care as much about Helen's life as an adult.

That, however, was the least of Helen's worries. Anne's eyesight was worse than ever, and in 1929, she had to have surgery to remove her right eye. So when Helen went to Washington, D.C., to speak to Congress, Polly went with her instead.

The US Capitol Building, which is the home of Congress.

The trip was a success, and Congress agreed to give $75,000 for the printing of more braille books. This was the first time the US government had ever supported a program for the blind.

Nella Braddy Henney
and Helen in Garden
City, New York, 1940.

In April 1931, Helen, Anne, and Polly went to New York. They represented the AFB at its first international conference of workers for the blind. Helen spoke before people from 32 different countries. After this, Helen would go on to make many international trips as an AFB ambassador.

Not all of Helen's international travel was for work, though. When they needed a break, she, Anne, and Polly went to Scotland to visit with Polly's family. In 1932, during the second of three visits, they learned that John Macy had died. He and Anne had been separated for years, but Anne was still very upset. She even paid for his funeral.

Helen's influence at home was growing. She became friends with President Franklin Delano Roosevelt (FDR), and she encouraged him and other lawmakers to help the blind.

---

what is an ambassador?

Someone who is a representative, often abroad, of an organization, country, or group of people. Helen was an ambassador for the AFB.

President Franklin D. Roosevelt signing the Social Security Act
at the White House in Washington, D.C., August 14, 1935.

In 1935, FDR signed the Social Security Act,
which gave unemployment insurance, retirement
funds, and assistance to children and the
disabled—including the blind.

One year later, Helen suffered her greatest
loss of all. Anne fell into a coma, and on
October 20, 1936, she died. Devastated by the
loss of their friend, Helen and Polly went back
to Scotland to recover.

Chapter 12

Honoring Helen Keller

Helen continued to spread her message after Anne was gone. She worked hard to make a difference in other people's lives.

In April 1937, Helen and Polly sailed to Japan. Helen carried a goodwill message from President Roosevelt to the Japanese people. In Japan, Helen gave 97 speeches in 39 cities, and huge crowds came to hear her speak. After her tour, there was a national call to help people with disabilities in Japan.

Helen and Polly continued their tour in Korea and Manchuria. Fearing the outbreak of war, the president of the AFB tried to convince them to come home, but Helen was still mourning Anne. Touring was Helen's way of handling her grief, so she continued to travel.

Then Japan invaded China. For the next month, Helen and Polly traveled in darkened trains, and Helen gave speeches in dimly lit auditoriums. This was because dark buildings were less likely to be targeted by bombs.

Travel abroad was becoming too dangerous, so the rest of the tour was canceled, and Helen and Polly returned home. Helen published another book, *Helen Keller's Journal*. Then she and Polly moved to Westport, Connecticut. They named their home Arcan Ridge after one of their favorite places in Scotland.

Helen

Polly and Helen during their tour of Japan.

In 1939, World War II (1939–45) began when Germany invaded Poland. When Japan bombed Pearl Harbor in Hawaii on December 7, 1941, the US entered the war on the side of the Allies (Great Britain and the Soviet Union). Helen had disapproved of World War I, but she agreed that the US had no choice but to fight now.

Helen wanted to help the soldiers, so the AFB arranged for her and Polly to visit military hospitals. Many soldiers had serious injuries that meant they would be disabled for the rest of their lives. Helen was a good role model for these soldiers because she gave them hope. Like her,

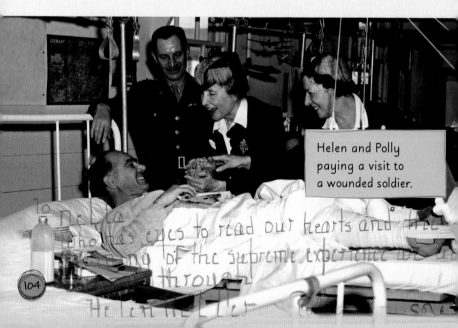

Helen and Polly paying a visit to a wounded soldier.

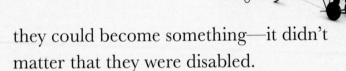

they could become something—it didn't matter that they were disabled.

After the war, Helen and Polly went back on tour. Between 1939 and 1957, Helen spoke before people in 39 countries on five continents and encouraged people to help make the lives of blind and deaf people better.

While on tour in Rome, Helen received word that her home in Connecticut, Arcan Ridge, had burned down. She and Polly lost everything, including 20 years of notes Helen had collected for a book she was planning to write about Anne. Helen's friends built her a new home, Arcan Ridge 2, and it was almost identical to the house it had replaced.

Alabama State Quarter, issued in 2003.

Helen's work wasn't going unnoticed. In 1953, she was nominated for a Nobel Peace Prize. She didn't get that, but over the next several years, she did receive enough awards to fill an entire room. Among them was the Presidential Medal of Freedom, which President Lyndon B. Johnson awarded her in 1964. (Years later, the US Treasury would honor Helen by putting her image on the Alabama State Quarter, which also features her name in braille.)

Once again, Helen's story was captured on film. Nancy Hamilton, who was a friend of Helen's, produced a documentary about Helen's life. *The Unconquered*, which was later renamed *Helen Keller in Her Story*, was released in 1954.

©A.M.P.A.S.®

Helen winning an Academy Award®, 1955.

In 1955, it won an Academy Award® for the best feature-length documentary film.

The Miracle Worker, a play about Helen's childhood, opened on Broadway in 1959. The play won the 1960 Pulitzer Prize, and it was later made into a movie. The actors who played Helen and Anne both won Academy Awards®.

In the midst of all this activity, Helen and Polly continued to travel. In 1955, they went to Asia. Over five months, they covered 40,000 miles (64,000 km). In 1956, they visited Polly's family in Scotland. In the spring of 1957, they went on their last trip as AFB ambassadors and, sadly, in March 1960, Polly died.

In October 1961, Helen suffered a stroke, which occurs when the brain's blood supply is blocked. Over the next few years, Helen had more strokes, and then she developed diabetes. It was hard for Helen to travel or even walk. She could no longer make public appearances, but she spent time with her friends at home.

In late May 1968, Helen had a heart attack. A few days later, she died peacefully in her sleep. It was June 1, 1968, and Helen was 87 years old. She had accomplished so much during her lifetime that every year since her death, people go to pay their respects to her in her final resting place at the National Cathedral in Washington, D.C. There, she is buried next to her lifelong companions and friends, Anne and Polly.

Helen, who had never feared death, was gone, but her life, like her message, will never be forgotten. In 1977, a war relief fund that Helen helped found during World War II was renamed Helen Keller International (HKI) in her honor. Today, HKI has more than 180 programs to help improve the lives of blind and poor people in 22 countries, and it presents several awards in Helen's name.

One of the most important activists of the 20th century, Helen Keller was and always will be remembered as an inspirational symbol of strength.

109

Helen's
family tree

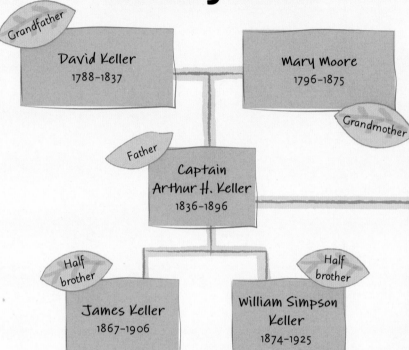

Grandfather
David Keller
1788–1837

Mary Moore
1796–1875
Grandmother

Father
Captain Arthur H. Keller
1836–1896

Half brother
James Keller
1867–1906

Half brother
William Simpson Keller
1874–1925

Grandfather

General Charles Adams
1817–1878

Grandmother

Lucy Everett
1828–1889

Mother

Kate Adams
1856–1921

Helen Keller

1880–1968

Sister

Mildred Keller
1886–1969

Phillips B. Keller
1891–1971

Brother

Helen was Arthur and Kate's first child together

Mildred married Laban W. Tyson and had three daughters.

Timeline

Helen Keller is born on June 27 in Tuscumbia, Alabama.

Helen gets sick with an illness that affects her sight and hearing.

Helen's family takes her to an eye specialist in Baltimore.

1880

1882

1886

1887

Anne Sullivan starts teaching Helen.

Helen starts studying at Radcliffe College.

Helen starts attending the Perkins Institution for the Blind.

Helen starts her studies at the Cambridge School for Young Ladies.

1888 1891 1894 1896 1900

Helen is accused of plagiarizing her short story, "The Frost King."

Helen begins her studies at the Cambridge School for Young Ladies.

Helen and Anne move to New York City. In the same year, Helen enrolls at the Wright-Humason School for the Deaf.

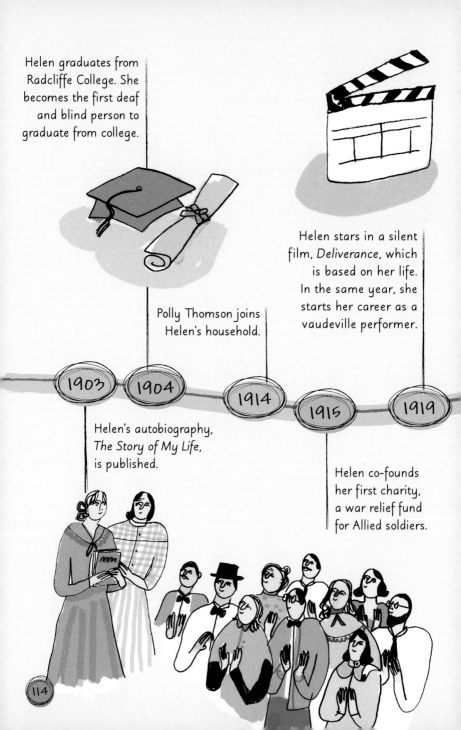

Helen graduates from Radcliffe College. She becomes the first deaf and blind person to graduate from college.

Helen stars in a silent film, *Deliverance*, which is based on her life. In the same year, she starts her career as a vaudeville performer.

Polly Thomson joins Helen's household.

1903 1904 1914 1915 1919

Helen's autobiography, *The Story of My Life*, is published.

Helen co-founds her first charity, a war relief fund for Allied soldiers.

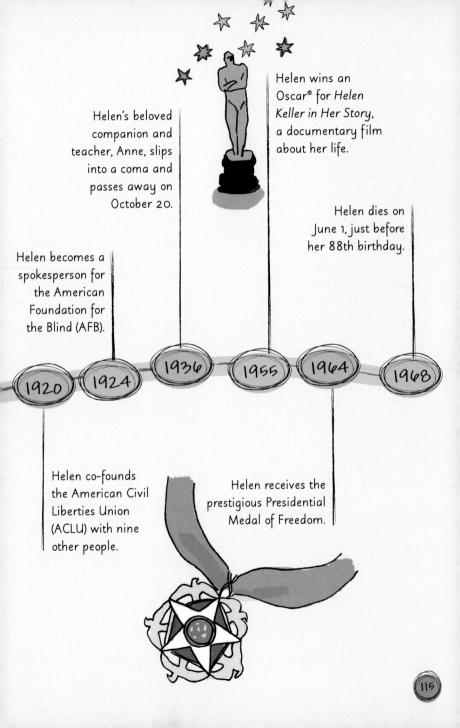

Helen's beloved companion and teacher, Anne, slips into a coma and passes away on October 20.

Helen wins an Oscar® for *Helen Keller in Her Story*, a documentary film about her life.

Helen dies on June 1, just before her 88th birthday.

Helen becomes a spokesperson for the American Foundation for the Blind (AFB).

1920 **1924** **1936** **1955** **1964** **1968**

Helen co-founds the American Civil Liberties Union (ACLU) with nine other people.

Helen receives the prestigious Presidential Medal of Freedom.

Quiz

 1   What was the name of Helen's childhood home in Alabama?

 2   What was Helen's younger sister's name?

 3   Who taught Helen how to read and write?

 4   What is the system that lets people read with their fingertips?

 5   Who gave Helen her first speech lessons?

 6   Which college did Helen attend?

 7   Who helped Helen craft her *Ladies' Home Journal* articles into her first book?

Do you remember what you've read?
How many of these questions about
Helen's life can you answer?

 What is the name of Helen's first, and most famous, book?

 What was the first movie made about Helen's life called?

 For which charitable organization was Helen an ambassador?

 What do you call someone like Helen who supports women's rights?

 What was the war relief fund that Helen helped to found during World War II renamed in 1977?

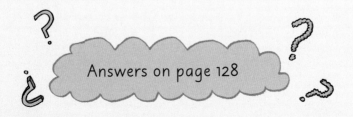

Answers on page 128

Who's who?

Anagnos, Michael
(1837–1906) educator and
director of the Perkins
Institution for the Blind

**Bell, Alexander
Graham**
(1847–1922) scientist,
friend of Helen's, and
inventor who is best known
for designing the first
working telephone

Bridgman, Laura
(1829–1889) first blind
and deaf person to learn
to read and write

Carnegie, Andrew
(1835–1919) philanthropist,
friend of Helen's, and
one of the wealthiest
businessmen of the
19th century

Chamberlin, Joseph E.
(1851–1935) editor of
The Youth's Companion
and friend of Helen's

Cleveland, Grover
(1837–1908) President of
the United States from 1885
to 1889 and 1893 to 1897

Copeland, Charles
(1860–1952) Helen's
professor at Radcliffe

Fagan, Peter
(birth and death dates
unknown) newspaperman,
Helen's temporary secretary,
and the man she
almost married

Fuller, Sarah
(1836–1927) principal
at the Horace Mann
School for the Deaf
who gave Helen her
first speech lessons

Gilman, Arthur
(1837–1909) educator,
principal of Cambridge
School for Young
Ladies, and co-founder
of Radcliffe College

Howe, Samuel Gridley
(1801–1876) founder
of Perkins Institution
for the Blind, and Laura
Bridgman's teacher

Keller, Arthur
(1836–1896) Helen's father

Keller, James
(1867–1906) Helen's
half brother

Keller, Kate
(1856–1921) Helen's mother

Keller, Mildred
(1886–1969) Helen's sister

Keller, Phillips Brooks
(1891–1971) Helen's brother

**Keller, William
Simpson**
(1874–1925) Helen's
half brother

Lee, Robert E.
(1807–1870) Commander
of the Confederate Army
during the Civil War, and
one of Helen's relatives

Macy, John
(1877–1932) writer, editor,
and husband of Helen's
teacher, Anne

Roosevelt, Franklin D.
(1882–1945) President of
the United States from
1933 to 1945

Spaulding, John
(1832–1896) one of Helen's
wealthy supporters

Sullivan, Anne
(1866–1936) Helen's
teacher, friend, and
lifelong companion

Twain, Mark
(1835–1910) pen name
of American writer Samuel
L. Clemens, and friend
of Helen's

Thomson, Polly
(1885–1960) Helen's
companion and helper

Glossary

ambassador
someone who is a representative, often abroad, of an organization, country, or group of people

antibiotic
drug used to treat bacterial infections

atomic bomb
powerful bomb that releases nuclear energy when it explodes

auditorium
large building used for speeches or performances

braille
system of raised dots for blind people to read using their sense of touch

braillewriter
sort of typewriter that prints raised letters in braille

capitalist
person who invests his or her money in privately owned businesses for profit

congestion
medical condition in which there is a blockage in part of the body

Congress
law-making branch of the US government

dean
head of a college or a college department

diabetes
a disease that results from too much sugar in the blood

embellish
to add extra details that may not be true to make something sound more interesting

FBI
Federal Bureau of Investigation—part of the US government that investigates crime

fingerspelling
way of spelling words with hand movements into a "listener's" hand, sometimes used by deaf people

graduate
someone who has an academic degree

grooved writing board
special board, placed between sheets of paper, with grooves to help blind writers keep their words even

heist
robbery

honorary
given as an honor, or out of respect, and without pay

honors
an award or symbol of excellence or superiority

immigrant
a person who comes to live in a country that he or she was not born in

legislator
someone who makes
and passes laws

lip reading
understanding spoken
words by watching,
or sometimes feeling,
the movement of the
speaker's lips

manual alphabet
different hand positions
to represent each letter
of the alphabet, used
by deaf people to spell

meningitis
serious illness in
which there is swelling
of the brain

Nobel Peace Prize
prize awarded each
year to a person or group
who has worked for
world peace

pacifist
someone who
is against war

plagiarism
using someone else's
words and claiming that
they are your own

poorhouse
building in which poor
people could live in
return for doing work

socialism
belief that a country's
wealth should be shared
equally between its
people, or citizens

sophomore
second-year college
student, or the second
year of college

southern belle
young woman,
usually with a wealthy
background, from the
southern United States

union
organized group of
workers that fights for
better working conditions
and fair pay

vaudeville
type of theater show
popular in the US in
the 1920s

water pump
device that pulls up
water from a well

stage fright
fear felt when talking
or performing in front
of an audience

stroke
serious medical
condition caused by
blockage of a blood
vessel to the brain

suffragist
someone who supports
women's rights

Index

Acknowledgments

DK would like to thank: Jolyon Goddard for additional editorial assistance; Romi Chakraborty and Pallavi Narain for design support; Jacqueline Hornberger for proofreading; Helen Peters for the index; Emily Kimball and Nishani Reed for legal advice; Sue Pilkilton for her expertise on Helen's life; Stephanie Laird for literacy consulting; Audrey Shading for additional consulting; and Noah Harley for serving as our "Kid Editor."

The publisher would like to thank the following for their kind permission to reproduce their photographs:
(Key: a–above; b–below/bottom; c–center; f–far; l–left; r–right; t–top)

7 Depositphotos Inc: Oleksandr_UA (br). 9 Getty Images: SuperStock (cra). 19 Alamy Stock Photo: INTERFOTO. 25 Alamy Stock Photo: The Granger Collection. 26 "Courtesy of Perkins School forthe Blind Archives, Watertown, MA". 28 Dreamstime.com: Georgios Kollidas (clb). 35 Getty Images: DEA / A. DAGLI ORTI. 39 Getty Images: Bettmann. 40 "Courtesy of Perkins School for the Blind Archives, Watertown, MA". 41 Getty Images: Bettmann. 47 Dreamstime.com: Sergey Lavrentev / Laures. 51 "Courtesy of Perkins School for the Blind Archives, Watertown, MA". 52 New England Historic Genealogical Society: Photograph of Helen Keller and Anne Sullivan, Thaxter Parks Spencer Papers, R. Stanton Avery Special Collections, New England Historic Genealogical Society. 54 Alamy Stock Photo: Art Collection 2 (cra). 55 Alamy Stock Photo: Everett Collection Inc. 57 Library of Congress, Washington, D.C.: LC-DIG-ds-05448. 58 Alamy Stock Photo: Granger Historical Picture Archive. 61 Courtesy of the American Foundation for the Blind, Helen Keller Archive. 62 123RF.com: gary718. 66 Alamy Stock Photo: Historic Collection (cra). 69 Alamy Stock Photo: PRILL Mediendesign. 73 Library of Congress, Washington, D.C.: LC-USZ62-78991. 74 Alamy Stock Photo: Historic Collection. 75 Alamy Stock Photo: Pictorial Press Ltd. 76 Library of Congress, Washington, D.C.: LC-USZ62-78762. 82 Schlesinger Library, Radcliffe Institute, Harvard University. 85 Getty Images: Bettmann (cra). Out of the dark : essays, lectures, and addresses on physical and social vision: Helen Keller / Garden City, N.Y. : Doubleday / Brigham Young University / Harold B. Lee Library (clb). 87 Getty Images: Buyenlarge (ca, cb). 88 Getty Images: Hulton Deutsch / Corbis Historical. 93 Getty Images: Bettmann. 95 Getty Images: Hulton Archive / Stringer. 97 CRITICAL PAST LLC: © 2018 CriticalPast LLC (b). Library of Congress, Washington, D.C.: LC-USZ62-32699 (cra). 98 Dreamstime.com: Robwilson39. 99 "Courtesy of Perkins School for the Blind Archives, Watertown, MA". 101 Alamy Stock Photo: Granger Historical Picture Archive. 103 Courtesy of the American Foundation for the Blind, Helen Keller Archive. 104 "Courtesy of Perkins School for the Blind Archives, Watertown, MA". 105 Dorling Kindersley: Gary Ombler / Royal Airforce Museum, London. 106 Courtesy of the American Foundation for the Blind, Helen Keller Archive: ©Academy of Motion Picture Arts and Sciences® (br). Depositphotos Inc: Oleksandr_UA (tl). 109 Getty Images: Hulton Archive / Stringer. 110 Getty Images: Bettmann (bc)

Cover images: Front and Spine: Alamy Stock Photo: Science History Images

All other images © Dorling Kindersley
For further information see: www.dkimages.com

ANSWERS TO THE QUIZ ON PAGES 116–117

1. Ivy Green; 2. Mildred Keller; 3. Anne Sullivan; 4. braille; 5. Sarah Fuller; 6. Radcliffe College; 7. John Macy; 8. *The Story of My Life*; 9. *Deliverance*; 10. American Foundation for the Blind (AFB); 11. a suffragist; 12. Helen Keller International (HKI)

All
New
People

Other Books by Anne Lamott

ROSIE

HARD LAUGHTER

JOE JONES

A novel by

Anne

Lamott

All

New

People

BANTAM BOOKS

NEW YORK • TORONTO • LONDON • SYDNEY • AUCKLAND

The author wishes to acknowledge the tremendous love and guidance of Bill Turnbull, Jack Shoemaker, John Kaye, Cindy Ehrlich, Abby Thomas, Ross Feld, Don Carpenter, Peggy Knickerbocker, and the reference librarians at the Sausalito Public Library.

This edition contains the complete text of the original hardcover edition.
NOT ONE WORD HAS BEEN OMITTED.

ALL NEW PEOPLE

A Bantam Book/published by arrangement with North Point Press

PRINTING HISTORY

North Point Press edition published 1989

Bantam edition/October 1991

Portions of this book appeared previously in California Magazine *and* San Francisco Focus Magazine.

Library of Congress Cataloging-in-Publication Data

Lamott, Anne.
   All new people : a novel / by Anne Lamott.
      p.   cm.
   ISBN 0-553-35278-4
   I. Title.
[PS3562.A4645A79 1991]
813'.54—dc20   91-22378
                              CIP

Published simultaneously in the United States and Canada

PRINTED IN THE UNITED STATES OF AMERICA

CWO   0 9 8 7 6 5 4 3 2 1

This one is dedicated to Bill Rankin,
James Noel, and the people of
St. Andrew Presbyterian Church,
Marin City, California.

All
New
People

I AM LIVING once again in the town where I grew up, having returned here several weeks ago in a state of dull torment for which the Germans probably have a word. There is green, green moss on the bark of the elms we shinnied up as children, when this was a railroad town. A thousand memories have returned in the past few weeks, odd and long forgotten, triggered by the sight of ancient houses, the smells of eucalyptus and the sea. They emerge as in those pictures we made when we were young, where you crayon circles and squares and patches of bright color until no more white paper shows, and then crayon over this with black until no more color shows, and then etch a picture with the tip of a paper clip—but by then you've forgotten where you put each original color, so that spidery Miró objects appear: red-violet trees, green horses, blue stars.

An old woman I've known all my life, named Angela diGrazia, calls hello from her garden, just across from the little white church on the hill. My brother started a fire in her kitchen wastebasket when he was four. Her old man and my father and the other men in the neighborhood, most of whom worked in the railroad yard, gathered once a year to stomp grapes, from which they brewed potent, battery-acid wine. I can remember her old phone number—GEneva 5-1432—but not her husband's first name. I wave to her but do not stop, partly because I'm late for my appointment, and partly because our conversation is always the same. First she complains about her back and the gophers, and then exclaims that there's never been any doubt about my paternity, although in fact there was, on my part. My brother told me every chance he got that mom and dad were not my real parents, and I believed him, partly because no one else in my family but me had wildly curly hair. "I remember the day your parents brought you here to live," he'd say with an air of wistful reminiscence. "Your mother was wearing yellow pedal pushers. And your father was a Negro."

Wildflowers bloom on the marshy fingers of earth that run down below the steps of the church. When the hillsides turn brown in the summer, millions of flowers appear in stripes: California poppies, leopard lilies, monkey flowers, buttercups, grass of Parnassus—brilliant white stars—and black jewel flowers. Black jewel flowers are dark garnet red, not known to exist anywhere else on earth but on these hillsides. You can still see San Francisco, Alcatraz, and Raccoon Strait, but when I was a child, the hills were shaggy and bare. My father took us on walks behind the hills, naming birds for us—juncos, robins, meadowlarks—and one evening at dusk we came upon a gypsy camp, their cars and wagons in a circle. The gypsies showed us small clay nudes—but maybe I've made this up. My brother doesn't remember, and my father has passed away. My brother and I caught tadpoles and frogs in the streams that cut through these hills, and my brother used to bring me to his fort up here behind a cluster of cypress trees, and make me undress for his cronies, who in exchange gave him baseball cards.

The old railroad yard is now the site of offices and condominiums, and I am headed there to see a hypnotist. My mind is an unholy puppet show. It is not on my side, and does not have my best interests at heart.

There is the matter of forgetfulness, how in my early thirties I already exhibit a worsening feeblemindedness; and how my mind is full of the forgotten, events that happened long ago and over the years that bred and feed my urbane derangement. And how I have told most of my stories so many times that it has become a way of forgetting.

One thing I know for certain is that my memories are not the same as those of my brother or mother or father; we all have our own version of what really happened, of how it really was. It is a *Rashomon* history. If you took our four versions and laid them one on top of the other in bands, as they do in sound mixing, you would end up with a song of my family.

I pass the field where we as a town burnt our Christmas trees on Twelfth Night. There would be a hundred trees or so, pine and fir piled like a massive haystack beneath the night sky, moon and stars. Then whoooooosh, it was lit and began to burn fast, really fast, crackling, snapping, with a roar somewhat like the surf, and it smelled like the essence of Christmas, a sharp thick smell like a pungent rain-clean forest, and we hooted and cheered at the roaring wild orange flames in the night.

My best friend all those years was a Catholic girl named Mady White who lived half a mile away, whose family I adored because they said "mann-aize" and "toelit" and "warsh," and because on Fridays they served tuna-noodle casserole or English muffin pizzas. Mady's mother wore her hair in a French knot, and you could push her pretty far before she would resort to the universal cry of motherhood, "*You* go to your room right now, and *you* go home, Nanny Goodman." Sometimes she would let us eat popcorn and tomato soup for dinner on Fridays, but unlike my mother she wouldn't feed the hobos. Once she gave a hobo who came to her door *The Power of*

Positive Thinking. Hobos still arrived in town when I was a child; they'd get on the trains up north, thinking they'd arrive someplace from which they could go someplace else, but our town was the end of the line. So they would come by our houses looking for chores, chopping wood or raking leaves. My own mother would bring them glasses of cold apple cider while they worked, and send them packing with a brown paper bag of salmon salad sandwiches.

My father went to see a hypnotist a year before he died. He and my mother were visiting friends in New York, and one of them recommended hypnosis to help him quit smoking again. "It was truly something," he wrote to me. "I was half expecting Lon Chaney, Jr., in *Inner Sanctum*—'Luke eento my eyes,' he would say, and then send me forth on a zombieatific quest for gopher blood or head cheese. But my man looked like a Great Gray Owl, with agate-hard eyes; there was a picture of him and his wife on the wall and you could see that just as the shutter clicks he is saying, 'No, I won't miss you, not any of you.' This look is what I would have expected to discover in the deepest recesses of my soul, but what I found instead was a soft tranquil pool. Afterwards, I went without smoking for nearly an hour."

My hypnotist is sixty or so, smiling and kind, John Kenneth Galbraith in L. L. Bean clothes. "How are you?" he asks.

"Fine," I say, and offer as proof a leering rictus of a smile.

His uncluttered desk and chair and the chair beside it, in which I now sit, are the only furniture in his office. On the wall is a print of a Chinese lion, the only decor. One window looks out on the bay, through trees.

"What are you here to work on?" he asks.

"Oh," I say, "anxiety, melancholia; fears of loss, rejection, death, humiliation, suicide, madness . . ."

He is nodding at me, kind and thoughtful, "Okay, then," he says, "tell me what your strengths are."

Squirming, fidgety, I finally allow as to how I can be sort of kind, sort of funny.

"All right then. You'll need to remember that later."

"How long is this going to take?"

"Altogether? Maybe a couple of hours. Let's begin." He asks me to close my eyes. "Good. Now take a few deep breaths. All right: now think of a color you really love, a color you find soothing, and breathe that color in and out, over and over."

I settle on chick yellow, inhale it, exhale it.

"Now, while breathing in your color, say to yourself, over and over and over, 'I am hearing . . . , I am seeing . . . , I am feeling . . . , but fill in the blanks, 'I am hearing—my voice, I am seeing—black, I am feeling—skeptical, I am hearing—my heart . . .'"

I am hearing my breath, I am seeing spangly black, I am feeling skeptical, hearing the rustle of leaves, seeing my own face, hearing the hypnotist clearing his throat, seeing the sea, feeling hungry, hearing birdsong, seeing our hillsides in winter, Ireland green, feeling relaxed. "Deeper and deeper," the hypnotist says, "over and over and over." After a long while, I am aware of an amniotic silence in my head, and then I am aware that I'm on the verge of drooling.

"Now," he says. "Beginning with today, I want you to go backwards in time, and ferret out the memories of pain: of despair, rejection, terror, shame. Freeze each memory, study it like a photograph, and then go backwards to the next one. Take as much time as you need."

The first moving slide appears on the screen in my head. I see myself lurching away from the home in Petaluma that I had shared with two couples in love, a home to which I had fled when my marriage broke up, a home so full of romantic gazes that I felt alternately like the lonely innkeeper and the court jester. Climbing down the porch stairs with two heavy suitcases, bolting for my car, consumed with memories of pain, staggering like Gabriela Andersen-Schiess coming around the track in the final lap of the Olympic marathon, where the pain and exertion are so great that they could have caused brain damage. I study this still with absolutely bemused detachment. I go back several months to the end of the marriage, in the ramshackle house on the Petaluma River. The water was so beautiful at sunset it could make your stomach buckle. We lived there for three years, my husband and I. The hills went from green in the winter and spring to golden yellow, Northern California in her blond phase, and the hay grows taller and taller, until you wake up one morning to the sound of the hay-cutting machines, which leave the hay on the ground in drifts, and then the bales appear, neatly stacked, golden blocks. By the end of our marriage we sound like Harold Pinter characters, clipped and malicious but ever genteel. Scenes from our marriage that even this morning sent a sickness rushing up my spine—but now I am blithely reviewing them as though I'm on nitrous oxide, placidly aware of the pain. I see our eventual aggressive indifference, hear our gratuitous lies, realize the great betrayal was being replaced in his heart by his work. Lacking the courage to live a quiet anonymous life, he chases down fame as an artist, and finds it to be a cold, beautiful woman who makes it clear he doesn't quite deliver, and I am made to pay, over and over again. Unfolding backwards through the years, I finally arrive at the hardest memories of all, the joy of falling in love.

"Backwards, backwards," says the hypnotist.

I am on Mount Tamalpais, twenty-four years old. A week or so before, I had finally emerged from the grief of losing my father, poking my head tentatively out into the world like the aged Japanese warrior coming out of the forest, desperate to know if the emperor is still in power. In town, I ran into the love of my life, a man with whom I had broken up around the time my father got sick, six months ago. We started talking and joking around, and he invited me along for the ride to Petaluma for cocktails with the couple who were our best friends. They were so happy to see us that we ended up staying for dinner. My lover had never before been so publicly demonstrative with me, and I mentally ran through the reasons I shouldn't start up with him again, but it was obvious as the evening progressed that he was back in love. When we went to leave, the engine of his car caught fire, and we had to spend the night with our friends. Clearly a case of divine intervention—God meant for us to be lovers again. And so I began to relax, and fell in love again. Our friends drove us home late the next morning, but we were all so relieved that my lover and I were back together that we stopped to buy champagne and take-out Chinese food and drove up the mountain for a picnic.

We are sitting on a knoll at the top of the mountain with what looks to be a view of the entire world. Over to the right is the deep-blue Pacific, and hillsides roll down beneath us everywhere you look, ridges and limitless trees, the bay gray-green and peppered with boats, and San Francisco as lovely as Atlantis. My lover appears to be almost sick with love and has never seemed so devoted, and our friends are singing the first lines of "What a Diff'rence a Day Makes" to us, and we're all looking bashful and goopy. Finally we are walking to the car, and our friends are looking at their watches, and ask us nonchalantly if they can drop both of us off at my lover's house to save time—they've got to get back to Petaluma—and I say Sure, and my lover says No, clearing his throat, and that there's a bit of a problem, and we all cock our heads nervous-sweetly, and I say, Don't worry, I won't *stay*, I'll just call a cab from there, and he looks stricken and finally blurts out that a woman is waiting at his house for him. I stand there on the mountain frozen by public disgrace.

I study this slide. Backwards? Backwards then. Except for my father's illness, I'm mostly seeing a sort of moving police lineup of boyfriends and breakups and the ensuing small breakdowns, and then I see a clip in which my father and I are talking heart-to-heart in his study. It is nighttime and we are sipping whiskey, I am twenty-one and sitting on the floor with my back against the closed door, and he is at his desk. He is trying to talk me out of beginning an affair with the married man on whom I have a crush, and who (as I confide to my father) is after me. You've had your married affair, he says, and it took you a year to get over. Didn't you learn anything at all from the experience? Because, baby, ignorance is curable, stupidity is forever. I hang on his every word. We drink more whiskey and talk about low self-esteem. We are unspeakably close, cronies, allies, family. He says that the clean thing would be not to sleep with Richard, and that there was happiness in clean. And I'm nodding, suddenly solemn and wise, and promise the both of us to nip this one in the bud. So when I do proceed with the affair, I lie through my teeth to my parents about where I am going at night and who I am seeing. The married man and I have a ball, and there is absolutely no way my parents can find out. Except that one afternoon there was a letter to my parents from the wife. I was met at the front door by my father, who was almost crying as he handed me the letter. My mother came into the hall looking at me with an expression I'd only seen on her face when she was watching Nixon on TV: Liar! Liar!

I study the three of us for a moment. "Backwards," says the hypnotist.

I see myself at nineteen in love with a man who was not particularly bright, but handsome and streetwise and cool. We had been sleeping together for three weeks or so when my period started, and it started just an hour or so before we went out to celebrate something at a fancy restaurant. I couldn't bring myself to tell him what was going on. He was not enlightened. He didn't like the smell or taste of women's bodies. "This is wonderful," said the therapist I was seeing at the time, when I called for an emergency consultation. "You've always had this disgust toward your own body, and now you've found someone you can share that with." She coached me on how to tell him, urged me to just get it over with, but God, it filled me with so much fear, fear that he would want me to go sleep outside in the hut until it had passed. And all through dinner at this fancy restaurant he made little sexy jokes about what he had in store for me later. I would laugh prettily and try to blurt out the news. I kept trying to tell myself that it was really no big deal, that it was okay to have periods, that it just meant I was a woman, and so on and so on, but I couldn't get a word out. He insisted that we go home to his house, and we held hands in the car and I tried to blurt out the first few words and I couldn't, until we were finally in his bedroom. "Oh," I said. "There's something I wanted to tell you." He took off his cuff links and started to pull his shirt off over his head and said to me, "Wait, wait, I want to tell you something first!" I nodded and smiled, waiting.

"Good news!" he said. "Clean sheets!"

Nineteen, eighteen, seventeen. There is lots of sorrow and low self-esteem but I also remember it as having been a time when my family was particularly close: we all fought against Nixon and marched against the war and boycotted lettuce and tried to stem the tide of developers who were building homes for rich people, building shops for tourists. I see myself returning from my only year in college, knowing more then than I ever will again. I spent the year hanging out with other bleeding-heart liberals who worked for McGovern and who would never ever drink Gallo or Coors, unless there was absolutely nothing else around. In my struggle to find out who I am, I take only philosophy and literature courses, reading most of the required books so that I could say I had read them, or because a paper was due, and I develop some rather gross intellectual pretensions. For a while I affect a slight and artsy lisp, and then move on to a scholarly, William F. Buckley stammer. I see myself sitting at my parents' dinner table telling them about the courses I was taking, and I see my hands near my mouth, gnarled with passion and emphasis, saying something like "The—thuhhh—thuhhh—

theeeeee *ma*trix through which we studied Thales of Miletus . . ." and my generous parents somehow manage to keep straight faces as I blather on and on; but after dinner when I'm headed upstairs, I hear them chuckle. I stop on the stairs and slowly turn toward the sound. My mother is saying softly, "The—thuhhh—thuhhh—theee uh *ma*trix," and I can hear that my father is laughing through his nose. "Dear God," he says.

I see myself a year earlier, my senior year.

I go to a tiny private high school for rich hippies, although I am neither, and one night at dinner I announce, sighing with poignant resignation, that, after all, the unexamined life is not worth living. My parents smile nicely at me, the same way my cousin Lynnie smiles at me when I complainingly remark that all these cats on Market Street keep asking me for bread. She peers into my face and asks, "They do?"

I look at that girl, at me and my pretensions, and then I see another moment in my senior year.

It is one of those Northern California dappled dawns, pink-blue-gray, and I have taken the early commute ferry across San Francisco Bay. Every morning I stop to pick up my best friend at her apartment on California at Larkin, and we walk to our little hippie high school together. This morning I get into her elevator and am joined on the second floor by a sweet handsome man maybe ten years older than I, who has soft black curly Jewish hair. I think I have seen him before, I think I have had a crush on him many times, or else he just looks like the man who organizes the action at peace marches, who introduces the rock groups on weekends at Golden Gate Park, who performs with the improvisational comedy troupe we go to see every weekend, who taught us how to clean up the beach and shorebirds below Slide Ranch, near Stinson, after the oil spill, who taught us what to say when we manned the phones at Suicide Prevention. We say hello and the door closes and then something comes over him, pain in his face, and he leans against a wall, grimacing, and I see that his knee is in spasm. I ask, can I help, can I help, and he nods and begins to slump to the floor. "I'm having a seizure," he whispers, and all I can think of doing is grabbing for his tongue so he doesn't choke to death, but he says, "Sit on me and hold my shoulders down." So I sit astride him and press his shoulders to the floor, and then he starts moaning and writhing, aroused and leering. "Ahhhhhh!" I shout and leap to my feet, nauseated with shame. I stare at the picture of this moment. I have never mentioned it to a soul.

Even years later I couldn't bear to think of it, and couldn't keep it out of my mind. It was one of the wormy memories that made up the House of Horrors ride in my head, where around every corner your cart goes flying into the mouth of the snake, or into the fire. But here I am watching it blithely. "Backwards, backwards," he says softly and I hear the soft rubbery knock as he taps his pencil eraser on his desk.

I am sixteen and in love with an older man, and it is a cat-brown night in San Francisco. I have told my parents that I am staying overnight with my best friend, but I am at my lover's apartment, and we have made hash brownies to eat the next day at Golden Gate Park, where Quicksilver and Santana will be playing. My lover is in bed and I am wrapping the brownies in foil, and nibbling at the corners and crumbs, just for the taste of the fudge. Everything is normal and lovely, and both of us fall asleep. Then I'm awake, the room is pitch black, and the cat is on my chest, and when I stroke it, its back is as long as a tunnel, my hand is going off into eternity. I bolt into a sitting position and turn on the light. The bed and the floor don't exist or maybe they do somewhere way way down below; I'm sitting on an infinite expanse of solid white air. My mouth is so dry that my tongue comes off my palate like Velcro, and I can't breathe. I'm having a heart attack! I shake my lover awake and try to explain that I'm dying, but I can't talk right—I sound like an Australian talking through Novocain and Quaaludes.

He drives me to the hospital and we are walking toward the emergency ward. He is grouchy and worried, and finally I realize that I'm just stoned from the brownies. I drop back, and when he turns to find me, I am lurking in the corridor like an egret, and I have to tell him I made a mistake: I'm not really having a heart attack, we can go home. And he looks at me with a hatred bordering on horror. "Ferret them out," the hypnotist coaches.

I am a sophomore at my hippie high school, where three of our students have died this semester, three out of a hundred and fifty, all three with socialite parents. One jumped from a window on Geary on acid, another walked into the sea, the third OD'd on smack in the student lounge. I am one of the few non-hippies, and my English teacher adores me; he is Bertrand Russell at forty, only funnier, and I live to please and astonish him. He assigned a difficult paper on *Moby Dick*, and several days later I learned that two of my eight classmates were using the Cliffs Notes, so I cleverly used the Monarch Notes and paraphrased its interpretation into an impassioned, possibly brilliant essay. Three days later, he read it out loud to the class, without saying who had written it, and my classmates cheered when he was done and I squirmed demurely, basking in glory and his approval until I saw him reach into his desk for a copy of the Monarch Notes, heard him read the passages from which I had cribbed my essay. I went brain dead. Rigor mortis set in. Class must have ended at some point because my teacher and I were alone, and he looked sad and guilty. I cannot see what happened next, I really can't, and so after a minute I go backwards.

I see the day when the last train left town.

My junior high is on the grounds where the dairy farms used to be, and I hate seventh and eighth grade daily but especially the nights when there are dances. I see myself taking it all out on my mother. I see myself punish her with sullen, aggressive laziness. After dinner, when she asks me to take out the garbage or do the dishes, I look at her like she just must be out of her mind. I remain at the table after my brother has gone upstairs to study, and my parents to the living room to read, and I wearily cradle my forehead in the palm of my hand, cursing my fate. Then I get up and carry the dishes past her as if they are limestone blocks for her pyramid.

Seventh- and eighth-grade dances, and gym: I pretend that my periods have started for about six months before they do, doubling over with monthly cramps so painful that I look like a man who has just been kicked in the old gwaggles. And one of the other mothers mentions these cramps to my mother one morning, and when I get home from school that day, my mother is waiting. And I have to discuss the ruse with her, which is all about desperate unhappiness, and I cringe, crying, the entire time.

I want to look and be like everybody else, but I feel so weird, so *other*. Everybody else wants to look like Jean Shrimpton or Cher, so I get my hair straightened and end up looking like a cross between Herb Alpert and the Shirelles.

Sixth grade is easier to take. Men are tearing down the building that contains the turntable in the railroad yard, the roundhouse where they fixed the locomotives, and they fill in the swamps where we used to raft, and build a Safeway, a ritzy hotel and a B of A. My parents march for civil rights. Our teachers show us *Reefer Madness* films, and we thoroughly believe the message—a mother walks in on her son smoking dope, and screams as if she had found him hanging from the rafters. Bad people, scabby and drooling, use drugs. So it is with a sense of horrified betrayal that I read an article by my father in which he describes an afternoon spent with his writer friends on a porch in Stinson Beach, drinking red jug wine and smoking marijuana. He has pulled the rug out from under me, and I march into the living room, holding the magazine, glare at my father who is reading a poem to my mother, and say slowly, "Daddy? You have brought shame upon this family." And he howls.

There is always one problem or another in having a father who is a writer. My brother and I secretly believe he can't hold down a job. Mady White has an uncle who "can't hold down a job," who stays at home all day (like our father) and paints toreadors and clowns on black velvet. I stand outside my father's study after school and listen with despair as he types. I also listen with despair when my parents fight in their bedroom about things that usually stem from there not being enough money; in my bedroom next to theirs I have to lash myself to a tree and wait for the storm to pass.

The allowance he gives her for groceries never lasts the month, and it is only by hook and by crook that she keeps us fed and clothed. I see her meet me at the door one day after school, in fourth grade: she is holding one of my white Mary Janes, but the strap has been chewed off and the rest is pockmarked with the teeth of our mongrel dog, and my mother is actually begging me not to tell my father— she's so stricken with guilt that you might have thought she had chewed up the shoe herself. She's whispering, she'll buy me another pair with next month's grocery money, and I am so ashamed of her shame, and so afraid of her fear, that I cross my arms and glare.

The hypnotist coaches me, "Earlier, earlier," and I look through a hundred migraines, the shame of migraines. Shame is where I live, shame and loss. I got migraines at birthday parties, I got one at the *Nutcracker*, one at the Grand National. I look through all those hours spent lying still in the dark pierced with white head pain, hallucinating. Once I got one at a movie theater with a family of Christian Scientists and I told my girlfriend, who told her mother. I thought they would take me home, but instead the mother whispered to me to rub my temples in a circular motion, and she showed me how to do it. I tried and I tried as the headache was building, expanding in concentric circles; the girlfriend and her mother both massaged their temples in circular motions along with me, all three of us staring at the screen like the migraine version of the monkey-see, monkey-do monkeys. But finally I had to get up and go into the bathroom and throw up, and then I lay on the floor with my face pressed against the cool tiles, and I kept scooting around on the floor because the tiles under my face would heat up the way pillows do. Then I remember them standing there in the doorway staring down at me, afraid, and that is all I remember. I was in second grade.

I can't see anything else for a minute—and then I see myself at Girl Scout camp for the summer, when I was seven years old, with a marble-sized growth on my arm, a vaccination reaction, and all of us girls are splashing around happily, whooping it up, when all of a sudden the knobby growth on my arm pops off into the water. The girl beside me screams, and all the little girls head for the shore shrieking, as though someone has spotted a fin.

"Ferret them out, ferret them out." I woke up from a dream at Mady White's house in first grade, screaming for my father, a dream in which the streets were wall-to-wall with people, and airplanes were dropping us bundles of food. In real life there was a book on the population explosion on the hamper next to the toilet at our house. My parents had explained what the book was about, and I picked it up all the time, and I'd look at the headlines on the back cover, gasping. I was six years old. In the dream I couldn't find my parents or my brother in the crowd and I screamed and screamed and woke up everyone in Mady's family, including the new baby, who cried at the top of her lungs for an hour or so. In the morning everyone was tense and exhausted, especially Mady's four-year-old asthmatic brother, and I sat there politely at the breakfast table, staring into a bowl of corn flakes, asking in a whisper for someone to please pass the milk.

It is getting hard to remember now. I see scenes of being caught by my parents in lies, or with stolen goods. I see myself with Lynnie

in her basement on the day after Easter, doing one of our nudie re-
vues, the dance of the veils—Arabian Nights—wearing only face
veils and veil sarongs. We have drawn concentric circles around our
nipples to represent belly dancers' brassieres, and we tantalize the
sultan—we whip off our sarongs, little Gypsy Rose Lees, naked as
baby birds. Then we hear my uncle, Lynnie's father, clear his throat.
He is in the doorway beside our neighbor John—who goes to Cal and
happens to be the man I want to marry—and they are both utterly
flabbergasted. We scream and cup our hands over our ballpoint-pen
brassieres, and both of us burst into tears. I study the moment, move
on.

I think I must be five years old or so, and my brother comes into
my room one night, anxious and sad. "They're coming to take you
away tonight," he says.

"Who is?"

"Your real parents, your mother and father. The Negro."

"No, no," I cry. "Hide me! Let me sleep with you tonight!"

He shakes his head wearily. "They'll only find you," he says.

I am in Children's Hospital, not yet four years old, standing in a
crib in a ward with nine other children. It is morning and I am talking to my parents, and studying seven black stitches above my right
eyebrow, where a cyst was removed while I slept. My parents are
beaming with pride. I am feeling very grown-up and sassy, and re-
port to my parents that one of the kids screamed all night, woke us
all up, and made us all start crying.

"That was you," says the nurse.

"No it wasn't," I say as if she is an idiot, or lying. And she says yes
it was; she had been on duty. The world drops out from underneath
me because suddenly I remember standing up in my crib, it is pitch
dark and perfectly silent and I am completely disembodied and
think I am in outer space, and I scream and scream for my parents.
There is a rush of humiliation, a sickening aloneness as my parents
try to mollify the agitated nurse.

I stay with this frame for a while. I haven't thought of it in nearly thirty years. But I'm stuck, can't go any earlier, and so return to the hospital.

"Are you thinking that you're there?" asks the hypnotist. I nod. "Are your parents in the memory with you?" Yes. "All right then. We're going to do a little visualization. I want the adult in you to enter the scene. The adult in you can be funny and kind, you said so before we started. Now go to your parents and thank them for raising you, and explain that you are old enough now to assume responsibility for the child."

Even in the trance I am filled with derision. This is precisely the sort of thing that gives California a bad name. But I swallow my reservations and walk up to my parents. We do not hug. I stand there shuffling. They look concerned, kind. I am the same age now that they are in this moment. It is too painful to see my father. "Go on," the hypnotist says.

"All right," I say out loud. In the dreamy trance I stare at my feet and tell them I won't need them anymore, that I am going to try to raise this child of theirs. I look up to see that they are nodding and it makes me feel shy and stupid and homesick. "Go to the kid now," the hypnotist says. "Give her a hand."

So I walk to the crib and stand beside it and look at the miserable child. Her sad face is screwed up with shame and I want to bolt. It is more than I can stand. Finally, though, I lift her out of the crib and sit down on a nearby chair and hold her in my lap. We sit there rocking. A long time passes; we rock.

"You didn't do anything wrong," I say finally, not out loud.

I try to think of things to say that are funny and kind, but all I can do is rock her and stare off into space. "That nurse was a shithead," I say. "You didn't do anything wrong."

"Now," the hypnotist says. "Play all of your memories forward, all the ones you've looked at today, and each time step in to give the younger you a hand."

So the adult me stepped into my own history, to help, and I went toward the memory of Lynnie and me in the basement doing our nudie revue, and the adult me was funny and kind, snappy, compassionate, there with the kid, saying, "You didn't do anything wrong," holding her, teasing her, getting her to relax. Then I went into the lake at Girl Scout camp with all those shrieking girls streaming and splashing out of the water, and I was there standing beside my seven-year-old in the water, making her laugh as I flailed about in mock panic, gaping and gasping at floating pine needles and twigs. And I was there with my eleven-year-old when she felt like a Russian hunchback at the junior high dances, me pointing out a boy whose fly was down and a popular girl dancing with toilet paper stuck to the heel of her shoe; and I was there in high school parties and classrooms, there the day I was caught plagiarizing the Monarch Notes for my paper on *Moby Dick*. "Hey, babe," I say to the fifteen-year-old who is cradling her head in her arms, crying soundlessly, alone in the classroom except for the mortified male teacher, "babe, I think maybe this guy didn't handle this all that well. And what was *he* doing, big UC Berkeley grad, using Monarch Notes to prepare for his classes?" And I was there with the younger me in bed with all those men, some cold, unfaithful, married, impotent ("Oh dear," I say to the twenty-year-old when a nearly impotent young lawyer is on top of her, frantically pumping at her, "it's sort of like he's doing his push-ups, isn't it?"). And then I'm there the year my marriage ended in the ramshackle house with cows on the hillsides around us, not able to help very much, just there in the room while she packs, letting her see that I am there, because the worst of it all, time after time, was the utter, abject aloneness. And then the adult me even slipped ghostily into the person sitting there in the hypnotist's office, like when a double vision slides together into one image, and I sat there for a while feeling sort of old and full of vague yearnings.

I opened my eyes a crack and smiled toward my lap, and suddenly remembered what it feels like to climb the stairs of a New York City subway station, about to go up and outside alone, maybe not knowing exactly where I am, only that I am not completely lost.

A minute passed and then I looked around at the branches outside, at the hypnotist's long thin hands, at my loud hungry stomach, at the lion on the wall—his cool yellow eyes—and listened to the passing cars, the rustle of the leaves.

One

SOMETIMES THE bay was choppy and gray in the cove, and sometimes it was so still that you could see the little town reflected on the water, upside down. The hills held working-class houses, and millions of trees, mostly cypress, maple, elm, oak, and eucalyptus. You could see the treetops on the water, surrounded in the reflection by bright clouds and sky. There is where the ferry slip used to be, where the trains were loaded and ferried across the bay to San Francisco, and over there is where the footbridge was that spanned the railroad yard. To the right are the long, low, weathered brown buildings of the boardwalk shops. Every year at Christmastime, a five-foot star of white lights appears on top of the grocery store; you could see it every night for miles, until it was taken down on the Epiphany, the night when the families gathered to burn Christmas trees in the railroad yard. There might have been a dozen or so arks in the cove, although around the turn of the century there were forty or so, and not far away, along these shores, were Chinese shrimping villages. A little white church sits on a hill overlooking the town and the bay, and behind it all is a mountain. In the olden days, a train crossed this mountain; there are fire roads now where the tracks used to be. On the other side of the mountain, there used to be missions where Indians sick with tuberculosis were brought to mend in the sun. In the reflection of the town on the water, sandpipers zip in tight formation, dipping suddenly, like ice skaters, flying now at an angle where their white undersides flit on the water like strobe lights, dipping again and disappearing for a moment. My family rented a small coffee-colored house next to the elementary school, below the little white church on the hill, above the railroad yard.

My father was a writer, and my mother an endless source of material. One of the stories *The New Yorker* ran began like this: "My wife gets these depressions." In it he describes her as having the movements and gestures of a rich European homosexual. She was quite funny looking, elegant yet deformed, and when she walked around the house wearing only underwear and one of my father's dress shirts, and lipstick, she was so sexy we swooned inside, my brother and I. But like Picasso's young girl at the mirror, her face didn't match itself: her eyes were dark green but the left one drooped, badly, and her right nostril was as big and round as an aggie. Her teeth were large and white and buck, and her hair was long and black and wiry, her skin was white, and she had beautiful soft-pink milkmaid cheeks.

She was a Christian, and not afraid of death or getting older. She thought of her body as being a car she would one day leave by the side of the road, and she wasn't afraid of things like snakes or driving across the Golden Gate Bridge in our Volkswagen bus, but she was afraid of revolving doors and houseplants. She always froze outside the revolving doors at the department stores around Union Square; she would watch people go in and come out, go in and come out, and she would begin to bob her neck slowly, like a turtle, to square and unsquare her shoulders and begin gauging the door like my young girlfriends and I did in the schoolyard when two of us would be turning the jump rope and the third would be tensed up, waiting for the exact right moment to dash in and pick up jumping.

She was secretly convinced that houseplants sucked up oxygen, somewhat like Thurber's grandmother who was convinced that electricity was dripping invisibly out of empty light sockets when the wall switch was left on. My father explained on more than one occasion that houseplants do just the opposite, in fact—they suck up our carbon dioxide and *secrete* oxygen—and my mother always responded, "Yes, in theory." She and her mother, Bette, had a falling out over this right after I was born, because Bette brought over three little pots of African violets to put on the dresser beside my crib, and my mother wouldn't even let them stay in the house. Bette found them in the garage, on the shelf where my father kept little glass jars of nails and screws and washers. My mother apparently thought that when the adults left the room and turned off the lights, the plants would creep across the dresser, high-dive into the crib, and smother the infant, like cats are said to do.

On Sundays my mother went to the black Presbyterian church in the subcommunity where the railroad workers lived, and on Fridays until I was five, she and my father went to Communist meetings in a huge North Beach basement. When I was five, John Kennedy came along and they stopped being commies and became liberals instead. On Sundays she walked to church all dressed up like a movie star, but with that crazy nose and drooping eye.

Sometimes Casey and I went with her, although it meant walking past the cemetery, which was filled with the parents and grandfathers of our town's oldest people and with soldiers killed in the two world wars and Korea. I recognized half the names on the tombstones, the names of our neighbors. Sometimes out of the blue my mother would go into the bathroom, close the door, and cry about the bombs we had dropped on Japan, and cry because Casey and his friends were growing up. While serving cake and ice cream to a dozen boys at Casey's ninth birthday, my mother paused, took a long deep breath, and fainted. After you passed the cemetery, though, you got to walk past the salt marsh, where once my mother and Casey and I came upon dozens and dozens of coots, ducklike birds with black heads and dark slate bodies. All the water had flowed back into the bay, and the coots were marching along the marsh's small muddy dunes, crying low laughing cries, and on the silt their footsteps sounded like rain.

My mother believed that God is our father, and we are all the children of God, and therefore we are all brothers and sisters. We were all one family whose home was the earth, and just as we had to love our cousins and aunts and uncles—even if we didn't always like them—we had to love everyone on earth. God knows it was sometimes hard to like Uncle Ed, who was always getting drunk and hurting Aunt Peg's feelings, and teasing me and my cousin Lynnie too much and making us cry. Once, when Lynnie and I were standing on either side of my mother at the piano, angelically singing all twenty-two verses of the English ballad "Matty Groves," Uncle Ed got the giggles, and as the song went on, and on, and on, Ed's giggles got worse, and he eventually had to leave the room. And another time, Casey and I got Aunt Peg three jewelry pins that were her initials, M for Margaret, E for Elizabeth, G for Goodman, pins that were at least two inches tall, studded with rhinestones, and she hugged us both to pieces and pinned them to her sweater. And she puffed out her chest when Uncle Ed came into the room, smiling in a funny way I couldn't understand—it was more of a grimace—and Uncle Ed stopped in his tracks, blinked, covered one of his eyes, and read the letters slowly, as if her chest were an eye chart.

Ed was the second son. No one had ever been as interested in him as they had been in my father, the family's golden boy; no one but Peg. Ed was a roguish sweetheart, Ed was a clown, but he could also be a terrible boor, and even my father would lose patience with him—until Ed would become as contrite as a dog and everyone would want to love and forgive and protect him again.

I did not understand the ties that bound Ed and Peg, and I worried constantly that Peg would leave him, would get a divorce. Hardly anyone got divorced in those days. Divorce was as stark as death. I did not understand why Peg would put up with him when he was drinking, although everyone liked to go around saying that she had the patience of a saint. Peg was a lady. People always sort of assumed that she had been raised in the South, the shy daughter of monied Texans, perhaps. She had a beautiful milk-and-roses complexion, long, long lashes, and she wore the most wonderful hats in the sun. I do not remember her ever having worn pants. She covered her mouth when she laughed, blushed easily, held her head high. She had gained fifty pounds when she was pregnant with Lynnie, and never took the weight off for any length of time, just as Ed could never stay on the wagon for more than a couple of months. I overheard my mother tell my father in their bedroom that she thought Peg took Ed in the same way—and for the same reasons—that Ed took drinks.

"And what are those reasons?" he asked her.

"She can't stand her feelings."

Peg made each of us feel that she loved us without there being any conditions on that love. (Well into my twenties I would still crawl into her lap.) I was so afraid she would leave Ed, and us, as afraid as I was that my parents would somehow end up getting divorced, that I turned into a hypervigilant little child, trying to make sure that everyone stayed in love with everybody else, a little bat of a child, a one-child war room. I tried to make sure that Peg didn't eat too much and that Ed didn't drink too much, and when they did, that everyone would forgive them, and I tried to draw Lynnie out in conversation because she was the shyest person I had ever seen and I was afraid that her rather rabbity shyness would cause Peg to eat too much and Ed to drink too much. Sometimes I was so obvious in my attempts to manage everyone's emotions for them that I must have seemed like a tiny stewardess on the verge of a nervous breakdown, and I would catch my parents looking at me as though I had cracked.

The only reason I could see for Peg staying with Ed was that he could make her laugh so hard. In fact, one of the first memories I have is of walking through Union Square on a hot summer day when I was five, Casey was six, and Lynnie was four. Peg had to go to the bathroom quite badly and the seven of us were scurrying toward Macy's so she could use the ladies' room there. All of a sudden Ed started making shusshing sounds, like running water, like a waterfall, and Peg started to giggle and to hit at him with her purse, but he wouldn't stop, and we all started laughing so hard that Peg and my mother and I all ended up wetting our pants. We had to sit in Union Square for half an hour, letting the sun-warm boards of the benches and the air circulating through the slats dry us off. We kept moving from bench to bench, and we couldn't stop laughing. My father and uncle and brother and cousin went off hand in hand and returned with cones of popcorn so we could feed the pigeons as we dried; and I can't remember before or since having been so entirely happy.

My mother insisted that God loved Ed just as much when he was drunk or boorish as He did when Ed was being endearing, and that we had better try and do so too. We really, really tried.

Having dabbled in the literature of the Eastern religions while she was in college, my mother half believed that you and God conferred before your human birth and chose the circumstances of your life—your station, your kin, and the triumphs and calamities you would face—chose them all as you choose a week's worth of breakfasts, lunches, and dinners while staying in a hospital. Maybe last round you had been a rich, blind recovering alcoholic in Minnesota, and next round you would need to be a beggar in Calcutta—but this round, you needed to live in a Northern California railroad town, you needed to be married to a novelist who could barely support you and your two strange children, you needed to have one huge nostril, but this side of the grave it might not make any sense to you why, before birth, you had arranged for this life.

My mother's religious eccentricity often drove my father crazy, although he was one of the gentlest men who ever lived. But at the same time, he relied on her continually to soothe the savage beast, as did my brother and I. You went to her when an ache in your heart was too huge, or when you had what she termed rat madness, and she usually said one of two things. The first was "Dwell in the solution," which was shorthand for something a Christian writer named Emmet Fox once said, which was, Do not dwell in the problem, dwell in the solution; the solution is God. Now, my father didn't believe in God, but he believed in the existence of the sacred, of the holy; it was pretty hard not to believe in anything in the face of Bach, or our mountain. ("It was good enough for the Indians," he used to say, and my mother used to trick him into going up there, when his spirits were low. "Get the kids out of my hair," she would say on a weekend afternoon, late enough in the day so that we'd eventually end up running into a sunset. We'd drive up the mountain and hike around, and my dad would walk along, mulling things over in silence, and by the time we were heading back to the trailhead, he would be happy, pointing out birds, and Casey and I would be lagging behind him, like it was the Bataan death march. Then he would buy us a Shirley Temple at the mountain inn, and buy himself a dark German beer, and the classical station was always on, and the sun would set in bands of rose and salmon, in the darkening blue sky.) And the other thing my mother would say—her other battle cry was, "Honey, it is gawwwwn." She brought this home from church one Sunday morning, courtesy of an old black man named Fred, who kept up a reverential patter during the sermon, saying, "Uh huh . . . oh yeah . . . ay-men . . . praise God . . . uh huh . . . oh yeah

. . . ay-men." And after this one particular sermon, he asked my mother how she was, and my mother confessed she was still annoyed, having lost her favorite sweater that week, and Fred looked at her like she was on fire, and said, "Honey? Sugah? It is gawwwwwnn."

My mother said it when we were unhappy about a performance—reviews, a little-league game, a spelling bee—or lost possessions, and it always cooled out the people in my family. So I tried it on Mady White's mother when she was shouting at Mady and me for having broken a pitcher. I held out my palms in a gesture of papal benediction. "Honey?" I said, "Sugar? It's gawwwwwnnn," and Mady's mother just lost her mind. By the time I got out the door she was actually braying.

Uncle Ed reacted badly to it once, too. You could never tell how things were going to bounce with Ed, even when he wasn't drinking. He looked like an angel and had fought on Guadalcanal, and except for that one time when he giggled so hard, he got misty when Lynnie and I gathered around the piano to sing our unrelenting ballads. He would sit on the porch for hours with Casey and his friends, teaching them to whittle miniature totem poles, telling them war stories, or he'd lift fat Peg into the air and spin her around, kissing her. But then, twenty minutes later, he would sour, brood, and glower and just generally pollute the atmosphere. One Christmas, after being sober over a month, he had a couple of glasses of wine with dinner. That was okay, he was being sweet and funny, and then all of us kids who were present that night went into the back room to play at knocking down a donkey piñata stuffed with candy and toys. As we learned later, Uncle Ed began muttering at the dinner table about a cabin he'd owned and sold at Lake Tahoe ten years ago—about how he'd sold it so they could get by the year Ed nearly totaled himself in a car crash, and he pounded the table and asked my father what he thought it would be worth today if he hadn't had to sell it. When my dad said, "Shit, Ed, it is *gone*," Ed leapt up, stomped into the back room, and picked up my brother's baseball bat. We thought he was going to hit us, but he swung instead at the piñata. The first swing missed altogether, and missing made him lose his balance, but my father arrived in the doorway just as Ed smashed the piñata in half, showering us with bright cellophane-wrapped candy and trinkets.

We didn't see much of Uncle Ed that winter, in fact we didn't see him again until February 21, the day before Casey's tenth birthday. I remember the date because we had a lame young white-tailed deer in our woodshed that my father found in the railroad yard, where it must have been hit by a slow-moving train. Our vet, who came by to examine it, said that if she was going to get well, she would do so within six weeks, and if she wasn't walking by then, she would have to be put to sleep.

The vet said that only one person should tend to the deer, so that she didn't get comfortable around humans, and that she should have a warm nest in the shed, and be bottle-fed three times a day. "It's Casey's deer," my father said, and none of us argued. Casey wanted to be a vet when he grew up. So the vet said to Casey, "Son? You understand your instructions? And try not to get too attached—because if she isn't walking by the end of six weeks, we'll have to put her down. If she is walking, she will be able to return to the woods." The vet consulted a calendar he had in his wallet and figured out that six weeks from the day would make it February 22, which was the day Casey would turn ten.

So day after day Casey went out to the woodshed with a baby bottle of warm milk and honey. Our idiot dog, an aged basset hound named Wayne, who smelled to me like old hairy glands, was forced to stay inside except for the twice-daily walks through the railroad yard that my father took him on, and my mother watched Casey tromp out to the shed and back, twice a day, watched this from the row of windows above the kitchen sink, and she cried and hid in the bathroom sometimes, and kept telling Casey to dwell in the solution, and that the solution was God. My father was quiet those six weeks, but he'd often put his arm around Casey's shoulder in a "Hey, buck up" kind of way and ask, "Any luck?" And I was especially nice to Casey and pretended I thought the deer was going to be all right, although I had read nearly everything Marjorie Rawlings had written and was nobody's fool.

When Casey seemed depressed and defeated by the deer's lack of improvement, I got so sad on his behalf that I would crawl into bed and cry; but when he was acting insufferable, filled with self-importance like he had the baby Jesus out there in the straw, I half hoped the deer would have to be put to sleep. Then I would feel such guilt, such a slimy fear about who I was, that I'd know somehow I was going to die.

From Casey's reports, the deer seemed to love him, but she wouldn't get to her feet. Three weeks passed, then four, then five, then six. On February 21, Casey asked our mother what kind of a solution was coming to pass. She said that maybe it wasn't the solution we had hoped for, and that this side of the grave there were many many things we wouldn't understand. But! Casey had been an instrument of God's mercy and love because, instead of the deer being ripped up by dogs and foxes in the woods, she had been nursed for her last six weeks by a young boy who saw to it that she was kept warm and free of fear, bottle-fed milk and honey. Anyone could see how badly Casey's heart ached.

He and my father were playing a lackluster game of chess when Uncle Ed arrived. I was at my swimming lesson at the rec center, but this is what happened, according to Casey: Uncle Ed, three sheets to the wind, had come to offer solace, having been told by Aunt Peg that tomorrow would be the day the deer would be put to sleep. He insisted that, since all hope was gone, there was no reason he shouldn't be able to see the deer. Casey didn't want him to, but finally it was agreed that Ed could poke his head in the shed door and look at the deer for a moment. So Casey and Ed trooped outside, Ed telling Casey his own sickly animal story from childhood, and when they got to the shed, Casey opened the door, and Ed lurched forward, missed the one-inch step, tripped, totally lost his balance and careened inside, where he crashed against a wall.

The deer leapt to her feet, wobbling for a moment, absolutely wild-eyed with terror. Casey's mouth was wide open and Uncle Ed was cursing, and the deer bolted out the opened door, past Casey, and into our yard.

Casey chased after her as she ran unsteadily around, and then Ed emerged from the shed hooting and hollering, and then our father ran outside. The three of them tried to sheepdog the deer back into the woodshed, but she stopped and looked around, sniffing the breeze, barely moving. Then she tore back toward the shed but kept on going, and jumped our dingy white picket fence, landing in old man diGrazia's empty field, and ran toward a corridor of blackberry bushes and cypress trees.

Two recurrent problems wore my parents down.

The first was money. My mother could make ends meet on what my father earned from writing and teaching if absolutely nothing unusual came up—if neither of us kids got sick, and the dog didn't get a foxtail stuck in his nose, and the cat didn't get into a fight, and if we didn't outgrow our uniforms (mine for the Brownies, Casey's for Little League), if no one needed dental work, if the tires didn't blow. Beyond the rent and food and utilities and clothes and gas, there were always bills at the drugstore, and at Sears, and at Mick & Pete's Mobil station, and with the doctor (because even when we didn't get sick, we had to go in for our well-children checkups), and

God knows where else. It was always day-to-day, hand-to-mouth back then, and it was erosive to my parents to go year after year without the big special things.

My mother believed that if marrying rich was what God felt she needed in order to get closer to Him, then things would have conspired to have her fall in love with a rich man. She believed that to just barely get by was His will for our family, at least for the time being. She tried to just accept things, to try not to figure out God's last name. But the fly in the ointment was that she hated to be cold. It made her stiff and edgy, and we couldn't afford to keep the house heated all winter and spring.

So she would go into the bathroom and cry, not wanting us to see her, and the three of us would gather outside the door, pleading with her.

"Darling, come out, we'll turn on the heat."

"We can't afford to."

"We'll get by, my love, come on out, we'll all bundle up and go collect driftwood. Build you a big roaring fire."

"Don't coo at me, Robbie."

"I'm not cooing. Don't be mean to me."

"You are so cooing. You're bye-bye bunting me."

"Mommy, it's not *to*tally cold today, it's only *cold*."

"Yes it is so *to*tally cold. YOU COULD HANG MEAT IN MY HOUSE."

The second thing that made my parents haggard was the sense that the world had ceased to be safe for children. We were taught not to talk to strangers, not to open the door to anyone when mom and dad were gone, not to take candy or rides from people unless we knew them really well—and this was twenty-five or thirty years ago, before so many lunatics were spiking Halloween candy and stealing children. The sad thing for my mother was that she believed too that

God shows up on earth as Christ, or Buddha, or Krishna, either to pass the word about love and peace and fellowship, or to inspect the damage that we the tenants were doing, and He or She most frequently showed up in the guise of the lost, hungry wayfaring stranger. Every thing and every one who cropped up in your life was part of the test, as of an emergency broadcast system. Did you handle it—or him or her—with grace and kindness and good humor? Did you love everyone as brother and sister? Even the winos and Russians? My mother really tried. She was an easy touch. Winos and bag ladies asked her for change to buy a sandwich or to make a telephone call, and she gave them dollar bills, believing that it was none of her business what they spent it on, that Jesus hadn't asked the blind man what he was going to look at after he was healed; He just healed him. Hobos came to our door, waiting for a morning train, and my mother gave them sacks of food and packs of cigarettes. When she found a Japanese family of three camped out by the salt marsh, waiting for money to be wired from Kyoto, my mother brought them home and made them stroganoff; they taught me and Casey to count to ten in Japanese and told us the story of the peach boy and the tongue-cut sparrow, and we let them sleep in our beds. A gypsy and her squalling baby came to our front door one night in the rain; my mother gave her a bottle of milk, some oranges, liverwurst sandwiches, and a package of Kents. We regularly took in battered women, although of course we were not told that their husbands had beaten them up; we were told that they had fallen down the stairs or been in minor car accidents. One woman named Nora came over again and again, always late at night, and Casey and I heard our parents soothe her, and once or twice my gremlins made me get out of bed and go see her, see her bruises and (what was worse) scratches. And then when I saw her at the boardwalk market, in daylight, in between tumbles, I had a sense of shy, mean power over her, and she always looked at me like I had just caught her shoplifting.

But one night something happened that shook my mother badly. It was around ten o'clock on a humid night in early spring. My father was in the city, hanging out with some other writers in North Beach, and my mother and Casey and I were on the porch, playing Parcheesi, sharing a pack of wild cherry Lifesavers. Our porch was enclosed with fine wire netting to keep out the insects, and the screen door was a piece of chipped, splintering plywood with a screen window and primitive latch, which was more to keep the door from banging in the wind than for security. It was a strange evening. The quiet dark was full of the songs of crickets and frogs and night birds, and our porch smelled of our eucalyptus trees and jasmine and my mother's cigarettes, and there was so much moonlight on the roofs of the houses below us, and on the roofs of the trains and buildings in the railroad yard, that it looked like there had been a light snow. Then, after a while, clouds must have blown in on the night breeze, because it began to rain.

We played our game and listened to the patter on the roof of the porch, and the frogs kept singing but the night birds hushed. All of a sudden a car pulled up outside our house and stopped. After a moment the engine and lights were turned off, and the car door opened, and a man got out; under the streetlight he looked like a cowboy. He began to walk toward our porch, and my mother got to her feet and said, "You two go inside," but we disobeyed and hunkered in the front doorway. You could tell that the hair on the back of my mother's neck was standing up; we listened to the heavy wet footsteps coming toward us, and to the rain on the roof. Finally, when he got to the screen door, she noticed we hadn't gone in and hissed at us to do so, and we did, leaving the door open just a crack. I went to get Wayne, our gassy dying basset hound, who was asleep on my brother's bed. I pushed on the crown of his head, trying to get him to jump down and run to the front door and be Rin Tin Tin, but pushing on his head just made the baggy skin go down over his eyes like a watch cap. By the time I gave up and went back outside to the front door, Casey was outside with our mother, and the cowboy's car lights were on, and then so was his engine, and after a moment he drove away.

"He wanted to use our phone," said my mother. "And you know what I said, I said no. Because I didn't want him to come in." My mother sounded about to cry, her voice was higher than usual, quavery, blue. Casey and I did not know what was going on. But when my father got home, early in the morning, we were asleep in bed with her, one on each side of her, and we listened to them talk and pretended to be asleep, until my father carried Casey and my mother carried me to our beds.

She said, Five years ago she would have let him in to use the phone. My father said, Times had changed. My mother said she didn't want us growing up to be afraid of strangers in the rain who came looking for help. She wanted us to love our fellow man. Otherwise, she wondered, what was the point? What was the sound of one hand clapping? My father didn't know what to say. The Japanese answer the riddle by asking, "And what is the sound of the rain?" Which is to say, Silence, until the drops hit against something, an umbrella, or a roof, or the sea.

My mother believed that God lit the stars and spoke to us directly through family and friends, musicians and writers, madmen and children, and nature—and not, as she had been raised to believe, through a booming male voice from the heavens. She and my father shared the beliefs that one must try to live in the now and be kind to everyone and to tell the truth, *unless* the truth was about Aunt Peg's weight, or that my mother's best friend Natalie on several occasions asserted that a girl simply *could*n't wear too much mascara, and the truth was that a girl could, and that poor old Natalie sometimes looked like a drag queen. But this marriage of my parents, which survived my mother's depressions and the constant lack of money, nearly blew apart when my mother told my father he said "you know" too much.

It was in the spring of 1963 that it first began to bother her, this tic of his, thirteen years after their wedding and two months after he ended a brief miserable affair with some girl writer who had a loft in North Beach. All of a sudden my mother noticed that after every other word my father said "you know," or at least so it seemed. It was all she heard when he spoke. As she told the story to Casey and me, a few years after he died, it got so that she was counting the you know's per sentence. There could be anywhere between six and ten.

She really didn't know what to do. If she mentioned it to him, it would be like telling him he had had bad breath all these years. He would be mortified, indignant. But if she didn't tell him, if she had to listen to him say "you know" every other word for the rest of her life, she would lose her mind.

She discussed it with Aunt Peg, who said it was all in the handling. If my mother told my father out of love, in a gentle and reassuring way, my father would see that he had this habit, of which he was totally unaware, a habit that the people who knew him found vaguely annoying, a habit easily broken. He would be relieved it had finally been brought to his attention. He would be embarrassed and ultimately very grateful. It would be, Peg insisted, a beautiful gift.

"So," my mother told my brother and me a few years ago, "I said to your father, 'My darling? There's this thing I need to tell you, that you do—that I'm sure you're not aware of doing. Which is that you have the habit of saying "you know," every few words. I mean, you say "you know" eight or nine times in each sentence.' And his eyes grew wide, and he turned bright red, and he was looking at me like he did when he thought I had drunk too much at a party—sizing me up in a skeptical way, and oh God, I knew, I had blown the marriage; how had I been so crazy to think that someone as sensitive and insecure as your father would be grateful at hearing that every few seconds he did something irritating? So much for, 'Darling, I have a beautiful gift for you.'

"He walked away from me. I called out that I was sorry, that I hadn't meant to hurt and embarrass him, and he turned, at the doorway, and said, in an arch and British way, Oh, hadn't I? Then how had I wanted him to respond?

"I said I had hoped that, after the embarrassment passed, he would be relieved, since it was something he was obviously unaware of, and something he could change.

"He asked, What if he didn't want to change?

"I looked at him, levelly, and then shrugged.

" 'Do you want me to start censoring myself?' he asked.

"I said I thought as soon as he was aware of doing it, it would fall away. After all, would it be like having to translate himself into French as he went along?

"He didn't answer. He looked too tired to answer.

" 'What if I do it,' he said. 'What if I black out every "you know" before it gets out of my mouth? *Then* what would it be about me that you'd think I ought to change?'

" 'Darling,' I pleaded. 'It isn't customs inspection; it isn't as though I have other things secreted in the lining of my luggage. I feel so bad, I've hurt you—but there isn't anything else I wish to declare—and we have to be able, along the way, to tell one another, for the rest of our lives, if there's something that is driving one of us crazy. Otherwise, we'll never make it.'

"But it was just excruciating, for both of us—worse for him though, of course. And I waited for him to retaliate—to say something about, I don't know, my jiggly bottom, or my . . . nostril, or to say that, as long as adjustments were being made, maybe it was time for him to mention that he didn't like the way I kissed.

"We were suddenly such edgy strangers, and although we'd been here before, I forgot that, forgot that it always feels like the new, permanent us. I forgot that somehow against all odds, the light always returns, that the light can't help but return, but it is hard to remember when everything seems so dark and smelly, like you had your head up your, well, never mind.

"All I could do was to force myself, at gunpoint, not to dwell in the problem, but to dwell in the solution, and the solution was God. And your father went off to lie alone in the mud, until his wounds could heal.

"The next few days were all stiff and hurt, and it was making you babies crazy, and I felt absolutely sure that we, your father and I, could never return to that innocence and trust—but I'll tell you, he didn't say 'you know' anymore. So I waited, and I prayed. Then Aunt Peg invited us all to brunch, after church the next Sunday, the Sunday before Easter, and at first I thought, No, your father and I would sit at their table like graven images and ruin everything for everyone, and then I thought, well heck, maybe this is part of the great solution.

"Sunday morning I somehow talked your father into going to church with me. We brought you kids with us—and I bet you don't remember what happened. But there was a part of every service right after we sang the Doxology where the choir sang a selection, but on this particular Sunday old Fred's daughter, Esther, was going to sing alone, a cappella.

"She was black as a person could be, shy, heavy, cherubic, twenty-five or so. She stood by the piano, closed her eyes, inhaled deeply, and sang the first crystalline notes of 'Awake, My Soul,' but then she missed the next note, and then the next—she was singing them both too high, and in the succeeding notes she tried to compensate, but instead she lost the melody.

"I mean, honey, it was excruciating. Esther had her eyes closed, her fists clenched, standing in front of us all, warbling away, way off key and out of tune, and tears were splashing down her face. No one in church was breathing, especially not me—because I thought it was all my fault somehow—I think I had a bit of an ego problem—but I felt wave after wave of guilt and self-loathing; my head was like a pinball machine, and its commotion had caused Esther to derail . . . And poor old Esther with the clearest, sweetest voice on earth wavered away and came to the end of the first verse. The pastor said softly, 'Relax, relax,' and Esther clenched her fists even tighter and started in on the second verse, and all the white people in church were in a wild frantic form of catatonia; you could have scrambled radar with our discombobulation.

"But then, the women in the first row of chairs, nearest Esther—the women who usually sang in the tiny choir, began to *whisper* the melody, humming it. You could barely hear them. And Esther's hands were still in fists and her face was full of humiliation, but she could hear the melody; and she sang it over the softest possible singing of the four black women. And I swear, it was like, when a whale is weak or bleeding, the other whales in the school swim underneath it, and buoy it up to the air, so it can breathe.

"And we were okay after that, your father and I, stiff for a while, but knowing the worst was over. At Peg and Ed's, all of you kids were terrific, which is to say, you all played out in the yard until the meal was ready. At one point I was talking to Ed, who wasn't drinking that day, and Peg was in the kitchen, and your father came over to my end of the couch and kneeled on the floor beside me, talking all the while to Ed about some stories he was working on.

"And the thing was, I'd secretly read one, the day before. He had left it out on his desk and taken you kids up on the mountain, and something made me read it. It was absolutely awful, whiney and dense, and I'd wanted so much to love it—to be able to confess that I'd sneakily read it, and that it was a jewel. But as it turned out, I had to keep my having read it a secret. I mean, what was I going to say, 'Darling? I have another beautiful gift for you'?

"So I was listening to him talk to Ed, pretending to listen, and then I looked down at my wrist and noticed your father was toying very casually with the sleeve of my cardigan, just sort of absently playing with the cuff, and I looked over at his face, but he was staring intently at Ed as he spoke, and I looked back down at my arm, at your father's long hand, a pianist's hand, fiddling absolutely unselfconsciously with the cuff of my sweater, just like you would fiddle with your own."

Two

ONE WINDY May my Aunt Peg left my Uncle Ed. He said he had been afraid that if she learned to drive, she'd drive away and leave him behind, and she did—learn to drive and drove away. Casey and I came home from our swimming lessons at the rec center one late afternoon and found Ed in the far corner of our backyard, scanning the bowl of sky in a daze. The sun, low in the west, behind the ridge, shone in reds and white through the treeline, through the dark green coop of eucalyptus, oak, and cypress. I was eight years old.

Lynnie went with Aunt Peg. They had gone to stay with Peg's side of the family in Carmel. Her family had some money but refused to give Peg any, to punish her for having married my Uncle Ed. Poor old Ed. He really was sort of a loser. How two brothers born two years apart could turn out so differently is anyone's guess, although they did have a number of things in common: tall thin bodies, round blue eyes, good (but smoke-yellowed) teeth, strong jaws, and long blunted noses. Their noses looked like my father and Ed had walked straight into walls before the clay had had time to dry. And they shared a neurotic tendency to become, in my mother's words, ethical consultants at large—in traffic, in lines, at concerts, wherever.

This ethical consultancy was especially hard on Casey; he was the one with all the dignity. We would be in the express line at the Safeway—Casey and his friend Henry, me and my friend Mady—when suddenly my father would see that the woman ahead of us not only had a lot more items than the nine allowed by posted express-line law, but she was also going to try to con the cashier into taking a check, in further defiance of the rules. So the ethical consulting would begin. It was completely out of character for my father but not for Ed. They always began the same way, by pelting the consultee with excuse me's until the man or woman understood that a consultation was in progress. So the consultee would hear, "Excuse me, yeah, excuse me, wait, excuse me—excuse me—listen. Excuse me, lemme just ask you something—lemme just, hey, listen, wait, wait, let me ask you something . . ." At this point the stranger would be looking at my father like he had a parrot on his shoulder.

"Lemme just ask you something," he would say, with what sounded like real interest. There would be a brief but terrible pause, and then he would cock his patrician head, point to the sign above that read 9 ITEMS, NO CHECKS and inquire, eagerly, sweetly, "Can you read?"

The difference between the two men was that my father was a critically successful albeit poor artist, and my Uncle Ed was a door-to-door salesman. As we would say some years later, Ed just couldn't get his act together, couldn't make much of a living, couldn't stuff down the feelings of rage, of existential dread. People like me, on the other hand, spent our teens and twenties trying to get our acts together and then were stuck with acts.

Anyway.

My mother had been in one of her depressions around the time

Peg left Ed. She walked around the house a lot, a lit cigarette hanging from her mouth, her left eye shut, as if it were swollen, to keep out the smoke. She talked to her best friend Natalie a lot on the phone, hid in the bathroom and prayed a lot, prayed for grace and strength, hummed hymns, cried. Natalie brought her gardenias and floated them in a clear glass bowl. Sometimes she brought her twin boys over. We would all pile into her station wagon and head for the rec center, where we swam all day and lay on the bleachers steaming, salty, sweating chlorine.

We had all just gotten back from the rec center the evening Peg left Uncle Ed. Mom had gone inside; Casey and I had been sent out to the clothesline to hang up our wet towels and swimsuits, which was when we discovered Ed. "Hey," we said and went to investigate, walking over a carpet of horse-red pine needles and then over another of copper oak leaves and acorns, over to the pear tree where Ed was standing. He looked down at us just as our father did when we finally caught up to him on mountain trails. His eyebrows were raised as if to say, "Hey, all right. There you are."

"Your daddy home?" he asked.

"Not yet. Mom is. Come inside, Uncle Ed."

Ed and our mother sat in the kitchen drinking beer, smoking cigarettes, and we heard Peg had left him. Casey and I went into Casey's room and simulated disfigurement: we smeared Elmer's glue on the backs of our hands to make them into the hands of the oldest person you ever saw, then carefully stitched our fingers together by passing thin needles underneath the top layer of fingertip skin until all four fingers of our left hands were stitched together. Then we pretended our fingers had bonded together in a dreadful smelting accident. We got along about half the time in those days.

Some time later my mother came in and asked if we would baby-sit Uncle Ed. "Take him down to the water," she said, "we're low on kindling." She looked at our hands and rolled her eyes. We gingerly pulled out the threads that bound our fingers together and washed the glue off with hot soapy water.

Ed and Casey and I trooped across the deserted railroad yard to the little liquor store in town, where Ed bought us a bottle of Delaware Punch, bought himself a half-pint of Scotch and a pack of Kents, and bought a package of corn nuts for us to share on the way to the beach.

It was sunset, red and golden pink, and the water was calm, white-green. Tiny waves sloshed the shore, and it smelled like salt and rain and seaweed. Casey started making a pile of dry driftwood while Ed went to sit on a wet boulder half submerged by the tide. There were a lot of birds around, mostly gulls and ducks, a cormorant or two, one pelican soaring out past the lights of the nearest buoy. Near the shoreline over to the east was a long, broad sun-carpet of red, through which egrets waded.

Then my father appeared. Casey threw him a small piece of driftwood by way of greeting. My father threw it back, waved to Ed, lifted me up, kissed me on the neck behind the ear, and, setting me down on the sand, took my hand and walked with me over to Ed's rock. Ed handed him the bottle of Scotch, and Dad took a sip. He handed me up to Ed who settled me into his lap while my father climbed up and sat beside us.

"So," said my father.

"Remember that friend of mine in the army who committed suicide by drowning?" Ed asked.

"Yeah, I do. But don't scare Nanny."

"Nanny? Does this scare you?"

"No," I lied.

Ed took another sip of whiskey, passed the bottle to my father. "He walked into the water and swam away from shore, way way out beyond the breakers, till he was too tired to swim back. Then, I suppose, he sank." We listened to the waves splash against our rock, swash against the shore. Ed put the side of his face down on top of my head, chewed on my hair. "I probably don't even swim well enough to kill myself."

We stayed on the rock another ten minutes or so, and then the four of us walked home. My mother was in the kitchen making tuna-noodle casserole, and Uncle Ed went in to watch her crush potato chips with her rolling pin. Dad made cocktails for himself and Ed and my mother. I went into the kitchen for some juice and saw that Ed was at the kitchen table wiping away tears. When he saw me, he got up and went to stand over by the cat box, which in those years was by the doorway between the kitchen and the back room. He asked my mother if she wanted him to take it out to the garbage and she said no, no, it could last another couple of days, things were so tight right now. Ed started picking a fight with her, asking how much could we save by making the kitty litter last an extra day or two. My mother just shrugged.

I was pouring apple cider into a glass, scowling. In my cold-stone heart I blamed my mother for everything. I blamed her when we were broke, I blamed her when she and Dad bickered, I blamed her and was ashamed of her because she was way too tall and had that one huge nostril and hid in the bathroom too often and cried, and because she bought gauze and adhesive tape instead of Band-Aids, and ointment instead of Mercurochrome. All the other mothers knew to buy Mercurochrome instead of ointment, or even better, Bactine. But she wasn't like the other mothers, who wore dresses and nail polish and smiled. No one else's mother wore her husband's shirts to town.

But I went over to her and burrowed against her. She smelled good and called me little duckie, and she handed me one perfect potato chip, as if it were a slide she wanted me to study.

Ed got an old newspaper from the back room and began stirring through the kitty litter with the slotted spoon. Our kitty ran in, sat down next to his box and watched Ed troll for cat shit, watched him like Casey and I watched our mother when she went through our bags of Halloween loot.

Above the cat box was a picture of Jesus that hung on the wall in our kitchen, rendered in charcoal and pencil by a young man from Lebanon. Jesus' hands were raised as if he was about to pray, but they were little more than the suggestion of hands; they looked more like gloves. My father always called the print "Jesus and the oven mitts."

Someone at her church had given my mother the print. My mother went to church every single Sunday. She had made the leap of faith. She believed that the answer is always grace through faith. She believed that the answer to Ed and Peg's problem would be grace. "There is *power* in the name of Jesus," she would say. And then Mady would come to play, devoutly Catholic Mady—and all hell would break loose. My beloved Mady and I might go looking for Mom, to see if she would drive us to the rec center or to ask if we could bake cookies or to see if she'd give us some money, and we'd find her out in the backyard shaking her fist at the sky, calling God a retard or a cheese-dick. Her pastor had told her, "You can say anything to God, He can take it," but this was apparently something the priests and nuns at Our Lady of Mount Carmel had forgotten to mention to Mady.

The fact that both Mady and her mother were such strange units did nothing to diminish my shame at my mother's blasphemous outbursts. I went through a phase in first grade where I was convinced my mother was part of a coven that met in our basement on Friday nights. It all began on a summer morning when I was getting ready to go to a classmate's sixth birthday party. I was wearing my lacy white Easter dress, a petticoat, little white socks, and black Mary Janes. Mady and her mother were going to pick me up and take me to the party, but first, my mother insisted, I had to eat a little lunch.

There would only be glop at the party, cupcakes and ice cream and candy and punch, she said, so she made me a hot dog with nothing on it to spill. But I simply couldn't eat and said so and was told then that I simply couldn't go. The hot dog smelled like death, but my mother wouldn't bend. When the phone rang and Mom went to get it, I took the opportunity to go out to the front porch, where I looked around, whistling casually, and threw the hot dog toward one of the rose bushes.

The second it left my fingers, I looked up and saw my mother openmouthed at the window, and it was like I was artistically placing the hot dog into the air in slow motion. My hand was poised, almost arthritically, like when you are playing horseshoes. And then I heard Mady calling my name; she and her mother were at our front gate. My mother burst through the front door only wearing one of my father's old shirts and a pair of underpants, bellowing, "JEEE-SUS CHRIST ON A CRUTCH."

I don't remember what happened next, only that I was in the backseat of Mrs. White's station wagon, staring blearily at the plastic Mother Mary mounted on the dashboard while Mrs. White checked the rearview mirror to see if the hound from hell was chasing our car. And Mady gazed at her mother with blissful adoration.

I felt about as low and ashamed as I'd ever felt before. My stomach ached, my heart hurt. I tried to block out the scene with my mother, tried to feel happy I was heading to a party. Natalie used to tell my mother you had to get out of the pit as soon as you could. You had to get out of the pit as soon as you noticed you'd gone into it, otherwise you'd start furnishing it. I mean, since it looked like you were going to live there forever, why not make it more comfortable?

I was better when we got to the party. There were streamers, balloons, a magician who pulled a live rabbit out of his hat, pin the tail on the donkey, little paper cups of M&Ms. All the little girls got toy diamond rings; there was Burl Ives on the hi-fi singing children's favorites. I was in heaven, I was the star, I was the clown. But Mady was cute as a button and rich, and I heard her mention my name to a group of giggling girls, and I saw the mother of the birthday girl scold her gently, and I heard Mady reply, in a friendly, dithery way, with her pretty, bee-stung lips pursed with complacence, ever so sweetly, ever so blithely, and ever so loudly, "But Nanny's mother's going to rot in hell for all eternity."

Casey adored Uncle Ed all those years. They used to go for runs together through the woods early in the morning, and sometimes they went fishing out at Bass Lake in the summer. They both loved Jack London. Ed taught Casey everything he knew about cars, and they rebuilt some engines together. My father gave Casey his first toolbox and tools, but it was Ed who taught him how to use them. All of us loved Uncle Ed but he and Casey had something rare. You could see it in the way they hugged, even after Casey grew up. They didn't hug like other men do, embracing and then thumping and thwacking each other's back as if to put out a small fire. Casey and Ed actually held each other a moment or two and then, almost as an afterthought, they kissed on the cheeks.

They had some fallings-out over the years, usually about Ed's drinking. He ruined Casey's eighth birthday when he arrived staggering drunk, with a present for Casey, a samurai sword bought in Japan at the end of the war. It came in a dangerous-looking, jewel-encrusted case, and Ed had tied a bow around the handle. He lurched into the backyard where the boys were playing tag, waving the sword and beaming stupidly. Casey looked like he had just bitten into a jalapeño pepper. Dad and I were watching from the kitchen window. Mom was putting candles on a homemade chocolate cake. We heard Casey say, clear and angry, "You show up drunk at my party. I knew this would happen. I don't even know why I invited you. You show up drunk as a bum. Uncle Ed," he thundered, "I'll remember this!"

Ed won Casey back a few days after the birthday party by showing up more or less sober one night with a small box wrapped in the Sunday comics. Casey was hurt, mad, shuffly, and didn't want the present, but Dad took him into the study for a conference. Upon emerging, Casey begrudgingly took off the wrapping to find a hand-blown egg covered with watercolor and spidery ink. It was a portrait of a black pirate's freighter sailing on seahorse-infested waters—blue, green, lavender water—flying the Jolly Roger, manned by peg-legged, eye-patched cats, one with a spyglass, one with a samurai sword, all shined on by a lemon-ball sun.

Jeffey, our cat, got kabobbed by a spike through the chest the month Aunt Peg left Uncle Ed. It was on a Saturday, and Mom was home alone with the ironing, the kitty, and our gassy basset, Wayne. She was listening to the Broadway sound track of *My Fair Lady*, ironing in the living room, no doubt with a cigarette hanging out the side of her mouth, one eye closed against the smoke, when she heard the cat make quiet peeping sounds. He was sitting in a square of sun in the kitchen, hunched over and bleary in that hung-over way hurt animals get. When she tried to pick him up, he screamed. He had a hole the size of a tennis ball in his chest between his front legs, surrounded by dried blood, and through it you could see his lungs beat. "Wow," she said. "Okay."

Clearing her throat, she went to call the cat clinic. She was told the vet was in the city playing tennis and would be back in half an hour. She called Natalie, but Natalie wasn't home, so she went back and sat beside the cat for a moment on that square of sun, clearing her throat. The cat was silent, trembling, dignified, so badly hurt that Mom thought the dogs had torn him apart. She went out to get her smokes.

Outside the kitchen window in what we euphemistically called the garden, little birds were singing. My mother hummed a hymn, the cat sat upright, perfectly still, purred, cried from time to time and trembled. My mother sat down beside him again, humming her hymn, stroking the cat's face, then got up, went into the bathroom and, with raccoon compulsiveness, put on mascara until it was time to go.

As it turned out, the dogs hadn't gotten the cat at all. Our vet said he'd misjumped and landed on a spike or stake—it hadn't gone through his back and somehow had missed the lungs and heart. The vet said we could come get him that evening.

My father hit the ceiling when my mother told him the bill was eighty-five dollars. He made eight dollars an hour teaching English at night at the local junior college: ten and a half hours shot to hell for a cat he hated. Ed had given the cat to Casey for his third birthday, but Jeffey loved only my mother. He had it in for my father, would wait for him to fall asleep reading on the couch and then nonchalantly bite him on the head. No wonder my father was mad, but, as my mother said, "What can I do?" My father threw up his hands, went into town, and got drunk. My mother stood at a window in the kitchen staring out.

Casey and I bolted awake when Dad came home from the city at three in the morning. He and my mother made up in their room. He was crying because Peg and Ed had split up. "It drives a sword through my heart," he said, "to see a family break up," and he cried in remorse because he'd been mean to my mother about money. "It's only LETTUCE," he bellowed.

When I woke up again it was morning, and Ed had come over for breakfast. Ed said he hadn't had a drink in two days, and Dad was pouring them both coffee while he cooked mushrooms in butter for omelets. Mom was in Casey's room helping him write a paper on the gold rush. I went to hang out in the kitchen with the men. Dad made me weak tea with milk and lots of honey. I sat in Ed's lap at the table, and we watched my father cook.

"Well, you're right, you know," my dad was saying. "I know I've never woken up in the morning and wished I'd gotten drunk the night before."

"I wanted to last night, don't get me wrong," said Uncle Ed. "Got a call from the Chinks who own the apartment complex. They said they gave the job to someone else."

"Baby, don't call them Chinks in front of Nan. And you didn't want it anyway."

"Chinese people don't like me."

My father shrugged. "They don't like me, either, Ed. I said to Marie the other day, 'Why is the guy Jerry Berman hired to help at the hardware store so hostile?' Not hostile, exactly, but cold. He isn't with the other customers, not so far as I could see, but with me, I don't know, you'd think he remembered seeing me in a gunboat on the Yangtze twenty years ago, tossing grenades into his little village."

"Where do I go from here?"

"It's Saturday, baby. Help me work on the shed, or help Marie. She wants to put in a garden. There's weeding and hoeing to do, or you and Nanny go down to the beach and get driftwood. We're always running out. And there's a minus tide at eleven. But don't let Nanny fall in is all."

"What do I do if she does?"

"I won't fall in."

"You'll go with me, then, girlie?"

We saw a fox-red robin on the way, and then, on the beach, cormorants, gulls, a couple of ducks, and a tern. We collected a pile of driftwood. Ed stacked a short, neat bundle of wood in my outstretched arms, then gathered up as much as he could carry, and we headed home. We stopped when our arms began to ache and sat down on a curb, with the wood on the street by our feet.

Dad had left all the breakfast dishes in the sink and gone to work in his study. Casey was in his room, working on the gold rush paper, and Mom was in the backyard pulling weeds. No one seemed to no-tice we were home. Ed and I dumped the wood into the box by the fireplace and stared aimlessly around the living room, looking for something to do.

"Want me to make you an omelet, Nanny? You haven't eaten at all."

"I don't know."

"Would you eat it if I made it?"

"I don't know."

"Would you try?"

"Yes."

"Come out and keep me company."

I watched him beat two eggs and cube some Velveeta, and I smelled the butter sizzling in the black iron pan.

"Your grandfather used to say, 'Think about what you are doing, not about what you are thinking,' " he told me. "Your daddy and he, boy, they used to go at each other. Mother would cover her ears with her hands, whimpering, 'Stop it, stop it.' God, I still miss them. And my kid, all the time. Yeah. 'The young will see visions, the old will dream dreams.' Oh baby, no breaks."

I ate my omelet alone in the dining room, reading a Richie Rich comic. The cat slept on the table in a patch of sun. Casey tried to snatch the comic book away from me, and we hit each other but didn't do any real harm. Sometimes when he hit me, he left bruises. I would cry, flailing away, and scratch or bite. He always won, but then I'd always tell on him. We could hear Uncle Ed running water in the sink. Casey rolled his eyes and pantomimed chugalugging, and I shook my head, but then shrugged, because I didn't know. Then Casey picked up my last big bite of omelet and swallowed it whole. I revved up for a tantrum, then didn't bother. I walked out to the kitchen with my plate.

The sink was full of suds. Ed, with his sleeves pushed up, stood at the sink with his head bowed; he seemed almost to be praying. I watched him until he opened his eyes and looked over at me. Then he looked toward the doorway and waved to Casey. I turned around and looked at my brother, who had his hands jammed into his pockets. Then I looked back at Ed, who was swallowing hard and squinting. "Ah!" he said, nodding pensively. "There it is, duckie. There's that clean plate," and I slowly, carefully held it out to him, as if I had brought him a meal.

Right before the Fourth of July, my mother, Natalie, Ed, and I walked into town to do errands. Natalie had been around our house more than usual. Her boys had gone off to Yosemite with their father for a couple of weeks, and Ed kept showing up in tennis shorts, swinging a racket he kept in a wooden press with four screws that were always gouging his legs, pretending he had come by to see if Dad wanted to hit some. Then he and Natalie would end up going to the nursery together or even (once that we knew of) up on the mountain. They dropped me and Casey off at the rec center one Saturday morning, and on the way there Natalie unwrapped a stick of Doublemint before handing it to Ed, and Casey looked at me sideways, inscrutable.

Natalie had an artificial hip, the result of a bad car accident, so as we walked to town we all limped along with her. She and my mother met before I was born, around the time Casey was learning to walk and Natalie's twins were beginning to crawl. They met at a commie garden party in Sausalito. Natalie was seated at a table, and my mother joined her at the invitation of a mutual friend. The two women found they could make each other laugh. They could engage each other, get down and dirty right away, and as they got tipsy, they fell in love in the way that women do—the miracle of finding your best friend, the purest, deepening relief.

After that, they often walked together along the shore; everyone called them Natalean Marie. Mom with that huge nostril, Natalie hitching along; Mom with her big white buck teeth, Natalie with her drag-queen eyes. Natalie became an aunt to Casey and me.

So there we were, walking along into town—me and my mother, Natalie and Ed—across a footbridge that spanned the railroad yard. The grown-ups were talking about the Bay of Pigs, and I was staring down at the trains and the tracks below us, the ties and spare parts in the flattened brown grass beside the tracks, the smells of oil, diesel smoke, and iron. I could hear the clatter and hammering, the welding, the whistle of the diesel locomotive, the rumble of passing freight cars; I could hear it in my ears in the muffled way you hear the ocean in a conch, because the railroad yard was still.

Beside the yard was the wild blue bay, filled with sailboats, ferries, fishing boats, woolly green Angel Island, Alcatraz, and the Golden Gate Bridge. I was studying everything intently because there was a funny smell between Natalie and Ed, as intangible as the sound of an approaching migraine. It made me edgy. I knew how lonely Natalie had been, and I had heard my mother on more than one occasion tell her she had to have a lot of faith, that she didn't have to go looking for a new man with her butterfly nets and dart gun; when God thought she was over her marriage, He would drop the right man right into her lap, and she just had to be careful not to stand up too quickly and let him fall out.

I held my mother's skeletal hand, she hummed her hymns, and Natalie and Ed walked behind us on the bridge. In my daydream, the sturdy footbridge that passed above the trains became spidery, rickety, swaying, more like a bridge of rope in a rain forest—any second it might break and I would be hanging by the fraying hemp just above the mouths of crocodiles.

Up the road a bit, across from the rock seawall, we approached Mady White's house, and I wanted to turn back so the Whites wouldn't see us. They lived in a small mansion with a magnolia tree in front that was nearly as big as our whole house. They didn't like my parents, who were former commies and middle class at best; and they wouldn't like Natalie because she wore too much mascara and was divorced, and they wouldn't like Ed because he drank. And since I was the fourth in this chain gang, they wouldn't like me anymore, wouldn't let me come over and comb Mady's long, straight white-blond hair.

They were a perfect couple, Mady was a perfect girl, and I didn't get what my mother meant when she told Casey and me we must try not to compare our insides to other people's outsides: I just knew that I wanted Mr. and Mrs. White to like me. I knew they didn't approve of my parents. Once our families were at adjoining tables at the local Italian restaurant. We exchanged pleasantries, and my parents ordered a carafe of red wine, which I knew was too much for two people. The Whites had bottles of Coke with their spaghetti and meatballs. After dinner, my father bared his teeth so my mother could inspect for trapped food, and I remember blushing, wanting to die of shame. Mr. and Mrs. White had to avert their eyes from my chimpanzee parents, who would next be raking through each other's hair with long shaggy fingers, rooting around for lice.

There were swallows on the road where the White family lived, and they dipped and darted through the air, blue-black on top, camel and cinnamon colors beneath.

"God, that's a big magnolia tree," Uncle Ed said. It was a beauty, fifteen feet wide, fifteen feet tall, in full bloom—big flowers opened like cups, white on the inside, rosy purple on the outside, with a scent like violets. This was the tree we climbed when I came to play, when I wasn't inside combing Mady's hair. I was in this tree once in the winter when I heard a migraine coming. I looked around, although there was nothing to see or hear, and I waited and prayed to the baby Jesus, "Please don't let me get one." Mrs. White was going to take us to a ballet matinee, but there was no way out; I was headed into that private white one-pointedness. The air was like sheet metal waiting to vibrate, to crackle like when we simulated thunder and lightning during the school plays. I started to cry, "Oh no, oh no," and climbed down out of the tree. Mrs. White drove me home, and my mother put me to bed. The room had to be black, and word went out through the house, "Nanny has one of her headaches." Everything grew silent, mountain silent. I lay frozen, waiting, holding on. My mother or father brought and applied and removed cold compresses. They sat on my floor in silence, with their knees drawn up to their chests, chins on their knees, doing whatever they could in their heads to make me better, to make me sleep, until, some hours later, I did.

Half a block away from the Whites' house, though, Ed's old slate-blue Nash Rambler pulled up, with Peg behind the wheel. She honked. Ed was walking next to me, Mom was next to Natalie; we all stopped and turned to gape at Peg, who gripped the wheel—grim, sad, beautiful, fat, a Gibson-girl madonna. In the backseat Lynnie waved to her father and me. Time stopped, it was like a dream. Ed's eyes got wide, and he cocked his head and bent at the waist so he could peer into his car. His girl wore one of Casey's old white T-shirts and white toy pearls; her mousy brown hair was in braids. She looked like an angel. Ed waved to them, wagging his hand like children do, waving as if to say good-bye, bon voyage, as if they were about to drive off down the road.

"I'll talk to you all later," he said, looking from my mother to Natalie. He rubbed underneath my chin with one finger, the way you pet a cat, and walked over to the driver's seat. My cousin and I waved at each other. Peg rolled down her window, and Ed leaned in to kiss her; then Peg slid over, Ed got in, turned to salute us and put the car in first.

Natalie turned to my mother and said dryly, "My, my."

We walked along the rock seawall for a while; the tide was high and hitting the rocks two and three feet below us, spraying us with cold green water, wild salty water, and the whitecaps churned and bobbed like crazy rabbits.

Panicked and full of free-floating guilt, I walked ahead of my mother and Natalie, who fell into a hushed, animated conversation I didn't want to hear. I thought for a moment I heard a migraine approaching like distant mosquitoes, but I didn't get one. They'd never been that easy to predict. Once I got one at a Hayley Mills movie with Peg and Lynnie. Once I got one when the Whites had taken a bunch of us kids to the county fair and then back to their house for Hawaiian Punch and popcorn. I called my parents in tears to come get me, but they were off somewhere. Forsaken, I lay down on a cot in the Whites' laundry room, waiting, waiting, waiting, hot tears trickling from the outside corners of my eyes into my ears, on to the pillow. I held my breath as much as I could and listened to the other children laughing, fighting, whining, popping popcorn. The popping sounded like they were using a jackhammer to clear the wax from my ears. But finally I got ahold of Casey. He came and got me, rode me home on the handlebars of his bike, and when we got there, he put me to bed and brought me cool compresses and sat on the floor of my pitch-dark room, waiting for Mom and Dad to come home.

Three   IVY GREW everywhere.

It surrounded the house and vines hung from the rafters of the porch. It was all crazily green. Beyond the stone steps were redwoods, pine, cypress, laurel robed in moss. Ivy climbed their trunks. There were three kinds of groundcover: ice plant, baby's breath, ivy. Through every window you saw leaves and ferns, moss and ivy, kelly greens, army greens, black greens, lime greens, heathery greens, and the red bark of redwoods, and the true blue sky breaking through between trunks and treetops. One day I thought I saw monkeys playing in the branches several hundred feet away, but they turned out to be the neighbor children, playing on the roof of their house, with the transparency of all those trees between our houses superimposed on them. In the long, boxy living room I stared out on the days and pretended to be captive inside a terrarium, or sometimes inside an aquarium, watching the fish swim by.

We were housesitting late that summer in the town to the west of our own. The house belonged to a man who taught at the same place as my father and who had gone to Italy for a semester. We had rented out our house to a visiting professor at the seminary and his family so that we would have a bit more money in the fall and my father wouldn't have to teach so many hours. I missed being on the water, but we were at the foot of the mountain. Sometimes when we walked around town and suddenly looked up, the mountain was there like Mount Fuji, white with clouds where snow would be. The mountain, the Sleeping Maiden, was a dark wild green.

My father couldn't sleep in the new house. He was tired all the time. He was in what my mother called an agitated depression. She was in a lethargic depression. Casey was hardly ever around, and I was terribly lonely. I had always secretly believed that I was the only real human and that everyone else was a robot, but that summer I came to feel just the opposite, that everyone was real but me.

My father was ranting all the time, mostly at my mother. He ranted about our finances, he ranted because he was fiercely disappointed in Kennedy, he ranted about his lack of sleep. This was a big one that year, his lack of sleep. When people asked him how he was that summer, he told them how tired he was and that he couldn't sleep properly, and they would say things like, "That's funny. I always fall asleep at exactly eleven o'clock." They really did say things like that, I heard it with my own ears. Then my father would rant that people were insensitive shitheads, that if people asked how you were and you said you were really broke, they wouldn't say, "That's funny, I have tons and tons of money." He ranted about the heat. He ranted about our cat Jeffey, who kept biting him on the top of his head. He ranted because Casey was never home, and because I wouldn't leave the house.

"Darling, it isn't my fault," my mother said. "She's going through a phase."

"It is your fault, though, Marie. It's unhealthy for you to be so afraid of running into people you know, and now Nanny's caught it from you. It's just beyond me why you can't just say hello to people and then keep moving. I say to Nanny, 'Darling, it's so beautiful out, why don't you put down your book and go outside. Get on your bike and go play in the schoolyard,' and she offers some lame excuse, but *I* know the truth. *I* know what she's thinking is, she might run into someone she knows."

I missed our house, and I missed the trains and the railroad yard and the beach, the crabs and the starfish, and I missed getting to see Mady White every day, and I missed our blackberry bushes.

One night I was lying in bed listening to the wind and the frogs. The night birds were silent. Then I was aware that Natalie had come over and was downstairs with my parents, and that they were drinking brandy and that there was a fire going and that something was terribly, terribly wrong.

I went in and woke up Casey and we sat huddled together at the top of the stairs, scanning the empty hall, straining to hear. Casey finally figured out what was going on. Natalie was pregnant. I did not know how she could be pregnant since she was no longer married. I really did not.

"God, you're so lame," Casey whispered at me. "Remember when Peg went away? Remember all those times Natalie and Ed went off together?" He was staring up and out the window above where we sat at the top of the stairs. I imagined a tiny diamond star in the space where the rest of the moon would have been if it were full.

Those three adults, Natalie, Peg, and Ed, were the people closest to Casey and me besides our parents. They were the people that baby-sitters were to call if we got hurt, which we often did when Mom and Dad were gone. Natalie drove Casey and me to the hospital a dozen times over the years. She taught us to play tennis even though she couldn't run around at all because of her artificial hip, and she taught Casey to ride a ten-speed bike even though she couldn't ride one any-more, and she got him his first binoculars when he was nine. She took me to a beauty salon when I was six for my first manicure—she was having her beehive dyed black as she did every month—and she gave me my first purse and my first tennis racket from the local salvage shop. She drove our dog Wayne to the vet when he had to be put to sleep. I can't remember a time when she wasn't in our family. She is in my earliest memory. In it I am sitting in her lap in a sailboat near Alcatraz, listening to my mother and Aunt Peg throw up off the bow. Everything was bright blue, the sea and the sky, Natalie's turtleneck sweater, my father's and Uncle Ed's eyes, but what I mostly remember are the sounds, the seals, the gulls, my father and Ed singing shanteys, my mother and aunt throwing up, and Casey with his fingers in his ears singing nursery rhymes.

Ed just adored Peg all those years. You could see it in his face when he watched her, and in how lovingly he teased her, in how hard he could make her laugh, in how often he tried to get sober, in how often he started to dance with her out of the blue. Peg might have just brought hot dishes in from the kitchen and set them down, and Ed would be coming into the dining room with drinks or the salad, and he would take her into his arms and dance with her for a minute. Then she left him for two months and he pined and cried, and at the very end of it he got my mother's best friend pregnant.

My mother kept telling everyone that everything was going to be okay. She kept telling us that we had to remember to live in the solution, not the problem, and that the solution was God, until Peg told my mother that if she said it one more time she would take a rock and hit her on the head.

Peg was in my parents' room with my mother one morning when I got up. She was crying. I got out of bed and went downstairs, poured myself a bowl of corn flakes and went out to the porch. Casey was reading a book, eating Sugar Pops one by one. Squirrels raced along the branches, leapt from tree to tree, and I listened to their chatter and to the blue jays screaming from the treetops, and over it all to the voices of my mother and aunt through the open bedroom window.

"Why can't she get an abortion?" Peg asked.

"Because she's a Catholic."

"But I have nowhere to turn, don't you see? I can't throw him out—he'll move in with her."

"No, it isn't like that. It isn't an affair."

"Well then what on earth do you call it?"

"They just went to bed. You were gone, you had left. And they just went to bed."

"I can't move away with Lynnie, we don't have any money. My parents won't give me a cent, and I won't move back in with them. It was awful staying with them this summer."

"Maybe they'll give you some money so Lynnie can get some help."

"They didn't give us money when Ed was being good, Marie. Now he's knocked up your best friend and they're going to help us out? Honest to Pete! They voted for Nixon!"

No one said anything for a while. The kitty bolted past as if being chased by a dog. Casey munched his cereal. We had a swimming lesson at one. I wondered if my mother and Peg would be done by then so that our mother could give us a ride.

"Maybe Natalie will die."

"Peg!"

"Or maybe the baby will die, who knows?"

"Darling. Something is going to happen, something is going to shift, before this is through, I promise. I don't know what it will be, but I swear, it is all going to be okay. I promise."

Casey yawned but didn't look up. He hated swimming lessons, the way most children hated piano lessons. He still couldn't swim. At the rec center they gave you a small flannel fish when you could swim well enough to go the width of the pool and do the dead man's float for sixty seconds—and the fish meant you could play in the deep end. I got mine when I was six, but Casey didn't get his until he was nine. This caused both of us to feel deeply ashamed. I couldn't bear for him to feel humiliation. He did routines to keep his friends from knowing how badly he swam. He made up characters who belly flopped and dog paddled and bobbed about. He jumped off the diving board holding his nose, and when he reached the bottom he pushed off so hard that he shot back out of the water like a killer whale, ending up near the side of the pool to which he could cling. Or he hung around in the shallower parts and pogoed from side to side while saying funny things. My father was not a good swimmer either. At the beach he walked gallantly to the shore with his shoulders thrown back and his puny washboard chest puffed out, his stick-figure body as white as the moon, and after a couple of deep breaths he would walk into the frigid surf and freeze, gasping when the water rolled over his feet. Then he would make banshee screams as the water went up past his ankles, and after a minute he would tear out of the water and back across the sand to his towel, where my mother in her bermuda shorts and the top part of a calico two-piece suit would say to him, "There, there, darling."

"Don't look at me," Casey said on the porch that day.

"I swear on the souls of my grandchildren, Peg. Everything is going to fall into place. Something will happen."

"I don't know how you can say that. What if Robbie had a girl-friend in this town?"

"Natalie isn't Ed's girlfriend. Ed doesn't have a girlfriend."

"Let me finish! What if Robbie had a girlfriend in town and got her pregnant, and she wouldn't have an abortion, and no one involved had any money, and no one could move away. And you knew that every time you left the house, you might run into her and the kid, plus you knew that everyone was talking about you . . ."

"How will they know it's Ed's baby?"

"They just will. You know they'll know. They're like bats."

"I know what it feels like in your heart. I know what the knife feels like. You know Robbie's had those affairs." I plugged my ears and sang a tune I made up on the spot, and when I turned around to look at Casey he was gone.

"Darling, I'll make us some coffee," my mother said to Peg.

"Can I stay here and rest?"

"Yes, of course you can. Are you warm enough? Let me close the window."

I looked up and saw my mother at the window, peering out at all the trees, the redwoods, the ivy, the pine, and then she looked down at me and waved. I waved back. Then I went and leaned forward so my stomach was on the banister and my feet were off the ground. There were spiderwebs suspended between the stalks of ivy like fire nets, catching tiny leaves and wind-blown pebbles, flecked with them like the beaded hairnets my Grandmother Bette sent away for to wear in her airy fog-white hair.

Peg had always been vaguely suspicious that Natalie and Ed were interested in each other, although as far as either of my parents knew, they had never been to bed before that summer. But everyone's favorite Uncle Ed story involved Natalie, and I suppose Peg had heard it more times than she cared to. It took place the month Casey was born, when Natalie was still pregnant with her twins. Ed and Peg had had an enormous fight about the Sears bill, and Ed went out to hit the bars on Main Street. Several hours later and blind drunk, he appeared on the doorstep of one of Natalie's best friends, a woman named Pat. Ed begged Pat not to call Peg and divulge his whereabouts, and then he went into her bedroom and passed out on her bed. She panicked, thinking that somehow against all odds Peg would find Ed there in her bed, so she went downstairs to the bar where all the liberal-commie-artist types hung out, found Natalie and her husband Gabe and explained the situation. She pleaded with them to come home with her, and they did.

So the three of them sat up drinking red wine and listening to jazz on the hi-fi until no one could stay up any longer, and Pat persuaded them to sleep over rather than to risk driving home. Pat made Gabe sleep with Uncle Ed in case Peg barged in on the whole scene, and she and Natalie slept on the sofa bed in the living room.

Ed woke up at dawn still somewhat drunk. "I lay there," he would say whenever he told the story, "very very sick. I had one of those hangovers where you feel like you've washed up on shore somewhere hot, and you lie there in the sand half-dead. I was lying on my side, facing the wall, when suddenly I heard a man beside me breathing; and I thought, 'If I lie here really really quietly, maybe he won't fuck me again.'"

Peg gained more weight when Natalie got pregnant than Natalie did. The whole thing was a mess. Ed was on the wagon, professing his love to Peg whenever she could hear, but she was wild in her betrayal and fear.

One day my mother made me go shopping for school clothes with Peg and Lynnie. We went to the Sears store on Geary, and Peg seemed sort of more or less okay, although mostly all we did was eat. We hardly found any clothes to buy at all. When we were leaving, we got to buy both popcorn and chocolates; usually we had to pick one or the other. We bought a little bag of chocolate stars for Lynnie and me, and a big bag of bridge mix for Peg.

She sat alone in the front seat with her candy, staring forlornly at the road as she drove, while Lynnie and I sat in the back letting stars melt one by one in our mouths, watching Peg eat. She was scooping out a small handful every few minutes and lowering her mouth into her cupped palm like an old horse nibbling a handful of oats.

When we pulled up in front of my house, Peg turned off the en-

gine and sat there crying. Lynnie stared out the window at a bank of
ivy, with her head cocked as though we were still driving along and
there were many sights to see. I could see the steps of our house out
the window. They were made of stone, so big and so steep and they
stretched so high, all the way up to the huge blue sky, and amidst all
that green, all those redwoods, all that ivy, all those pines and eucalyptus flanking and partially shading the stairs, that they looked
like they might be the stairs of a massive Mayan temple.

My mother made a pot of tea for Peg and herself, cocoa for Lynnie
and me, and sent us outside to play. We did not talk about her parents or Natalie, we didn't talk much at all, and when we did it was
about my cat and her dog, Jeffey and Sarah-Jane. We finished our cocoa and then sat on the lowest branch of a cypress and kept an eye on
the tiny figures of our mothers sitting together huddled on the couch
inside.

That night at dinner my father asked my mother what they had
been talking about all that time, and my mother told us about a sermon our pastor James had given recently. "What he said was that
when all is lost and the center will not hold, that you do die an existential death. Like when someone dies or leaves you or in some other
way the whole bottom just drops out. It's like when Mary went to the
tomb and the body of Christ was missing and suddenly her center
wouldn't hold. All of a sudden she didn't know for sure if any of it
had happened. She didn't know what end was up. And James said
that when you're hurt that badly, you do die, sort of, as a means of
survival. And you lie there and you lie there in your grief for as long
as it takes, until finally, finally life can pull you back into itself; as if
it could give you its hands and pull you to your feet, so that you can
totter along again."

"What did Peg say?"

"Nothing. She just cries."

"Ed is a mess."

"Is he drinking yet?"

"He can't. He's on Antabuse. He's going to A.A. meetings. But his head is filled with guilt and self-loathing and fear, and what is he supposed to do, promise he'll never want to see the kid, the baby? His head is really troubled. It's like when Jeffey had that awful case of earmites."

"We just really have to live in the solution."

"Lambie, I think that maybe everyone is beginning to tire of hearing you say that. You've said it maybe fifty times since all this broke, and I know you mean well . . ."

"Oh go to hell," my mother said, and I flushed with fear for her to have said this, and she got to her feet, her cheeks flushed, her nostrils flaring. I felt a stab of pain watching her one big nostril flare. It looked like something a fish would have, not exactly a gill. Then she stomped off to the kitchen. My father rolled his eyes wearily and put his napkin down. "You kids finish your dinner," he said. "And no monkey business." We looked at each other blankly when he left. Then we wrapped our peas up in our napkins, stuck them in our pockets, and finished off the last of our meat loaf.

Ed came over the next morning at breakfast, looking well, as he always did when he was on the wagon. He sat with us at the breakfast table, refusing our offers of waffles, but getting himself a cup of coffee from the kitchen. He was wearing washed-out dark blue cords, and the chamois shirt we gave him last Christmas, faded dark green. And black zoris. He was in his early thirties at the time, although in my memory he seems much older. "Hey Case," he said. "Hey Nanny beans. You both hear what's going on?" Casey and I nodded and tried to look wise. Ed very slowly raised his head until he could look at the ceiling, as if maybe some sort of an answer was there. "How is Natalie?" he asked.

"She's okay," said my mother. "Sort of lost. But she's quit smoking."

"That's good."

"The twins won't talk about what's going on, except that she hears them talking to each other about maybe moving in with their father, who in fact doesn't want them, or at any rate his second wife doesn't want them."

"God."

"Plus she's heard them plot your death."

Ed nodded pleasantly. "I guess they probably deserve to."

"Oh Ed," said my father. "Give yourself a break."

"This is not my finest hour."

"Well what was, then? 'The paths of glory lead but to the grave.' This is just very human stuff. Go easy on yourself."

"Robbie, remember when Casey had just turned two, and there was that scene with the ink? Remember, Marie?"

"No. Was I there?"

"I remember," said Casey.

"How could you possibly remember that far back?"

"I just do."

"You were out of it, Marie—Nanny'd only been home a week; you were both upstairs asleep. It was in the late afternoon, and old man diGrazia came by with a bottle of his latest dago red. Me and Robbie'd been there for the grape stomp, and he brought us a bottle, or maybe a couple, I don't remember. But anyway, the three of us were killing a bottle when all of sudden Casey came out of Robbie's study with ink all over his hands and arms and legs, jet-black India ink. He'd been being so quiet and good, we assumed he was in there crayoning. And he said in a quiet and solemn voice, 'There's a mess in the study. It's a big mess. And it's my mess.'"

Casey tittered into his chest. He looked exactly like the early pictures of Ed, with the same cowlick, the same black brows, deep-set eyes, earnest concern, the same big ears and clever fingers.

"And that's how I'm feeling now," said Ed. "It's a big mess. And it's my mess. But at least I'm sober. Maybe that'll help. It sure as hell won't hurt."

"You going to those meetings?" my father asked.

"Yeah."

"How are they?"

Ed let his head fall forward on to his chest, and snored. Then he straightened up. "Shit, man. They talk about sobriety, and to me it's like hearing about the sun during an ice age. But my way isn't working. So I don't know."

He looked so healthy. His color was good and he was calm, if chagrined, and I thought that maybe this, Ed being on the wagon, was the solution my mother kept talking about. He and Casey excused themselves from the breakfast table and spent the rest of the morning in Casey's room, working on a model airplane. My father disappeared into his study, and we heard him typing away.

"What are you going to do today, darling?" my mother asked me.

"I don't know."

"Will you help me with the dishes?"

"Okay. Maybe Lynnie can play today."

"Lynnie's got ballet all morning. Why don't you come into town with me and do errands. It would make life easier for me."

"How come?"

"Because I feel like everyone's looking at me," she said.

"But they'll look at you anyway, even if I'm there."

"But I wouldn't be scared if you were there."

"Okay."

Old man diGrazia was browsing at the produce bins when we arrived at the grocery store. He was glumly studying the avocados. I wondered if he knew about Ed and Natalie. My father said everyone would guess because Natalie and Ed had gone into a bar together a few times when Peg was gone, and now Peg went around town looking like she had been crying or was about to, and Natalie's stomach was beginning to show. My mother reached for an avocado and old man diGrazia gaped at her as if she had just burped. His pants were belted nearly at the sternum and appeared to be swallowing up what was left of his trunk, like a boa constrictor. I stared. You could almost imagine the jaw hinges of the trousers opening wider, taking in more of old man diGrazia's chest. He seemed angry.

My mother asked timidly, "Is this the exact avocado you've had your eye on?"

He nodded, staring at his well-shined shoes.

"Take it," she said. "Honest. Please."

He squinted at her and then turned away, terribly depressed.

"I'd rather be mad," he said.

"I know," she said. "I get it."

Then the old man reached for the avocado, wrapped his long bird-bone fingers around it, placing it gently in his cart. He turned to go.

"I'm still mad," he said.

"Does he know?" I asked my mother.

"God only knows."

My friend Wendy Harper's mother was flirting with the butcher over at the meat counter. She was large, on her way to obese, and she always wore low-cut muumuus that made her breasts look like someone's bottom. All through my childhood she would catch me and press me into her big clammy moist bosom. God, I hated it. I tiptoed out of the store and sat on the curb outside to wait for my mother, drawing in the dirt with a Popsicle stick. I got up to see from outside the market if my mother was in line yet—she hadn't had much to buy—and was promptly ambushed by Mrs. Harper, who set down her bag of groceries and pulled me into her monstrous yawning cleavage.

After leaving the market my mother and I went to pick up my father's shirts at the cleaners. She had refused to starch and iron his shirts ever since we had this extra money from renting out our real home. We stood there waiting to be helped. There were people ahead of us, but no one I knew. I recognized most of the families whose last names were written in sloppy black felt pen on the blue paper bundles of shirts. All of them were going to talk about us behind our backs—I knew that from now on people at the rec center or the library or the post office would stop in mid-conversation when anyone from our family drew near. My mother was humming a hymn softly, seeming to daydream. We were holding hands.

The McGees had two bundles of shirts to pick up here. They lived in an old stone house on the road that ran along the railroad tracks. They had a Newfoundland and a garden full of roses and tulips, daffodils in the spring. In the winter the whole family went up to Tahoe and skied. The father was very jolly and in late summer he wore lederhosen. I wanted my father to wear lederhosen, and when I asked him if he would buy some, he said, "Later, darling." I wanted him to be a jolly lederhosen kind of guy, my skinny leftist dad with his moon-white pterodactyl legs.

On top of the McGees' bundles were the shirts for the Nathans. They were Catholic and had six children who went off in packs with the other Catholic children on Tuesday afternoons to catechism class. They pretended to love to go, to make us feel bad. The Otters had a pool. Mr. Otter was an attorney and had three bundles of shirts here. They lived on the hillside above the little white church, and his daughter had the best slumber parties because we got to go swimming in the dark with only the pool lights on, when the air outside was cold and the aqua blue water hot when you first jumped in. Mr. Pinole only had one bundle of shirts. I knew he must have to drop them off and pick them up himself. His wife Adelaide drank so much that a couple of times she was discovered passed out on the road above their house before noon, making a break for it. On Saturdays my girlfriends and sometimes Lynnie and I would hastily paint pictures and take them around the neighborhood, asking people if they were interested in children's art. How could you say no? They would give us a nickel or a dime, and say how lovely they were, our watercolor pictures of trains and the railroad yard, or boats on the bay, or deer and raccoon on the mountain. "Here's one that might interest you," we would say, and show them a picture of the Golden Gate Bridge, cars of every color on it, sailboats and freighters down below, sloppy V's for flying gulls. Adelaide Pinole would often give us a whole dollar after getting up unsteadily and lurching around the house looking for her purse. We were shameless. We called her Aunt Adelaide. Sometimes Mr. Pinole would rush in while we were there, wiping oil and grime off his hands with rags that smelled of kerosene, and shoo us out of the kitchen. Aunt Adelaide would sit there looking like we had all just been busted. "Have pity on her," Mr. Pinole would beseech us, handing us our paintings at the door. "Have pity on her."

My mother called Natalie from the dry cleaners' phone and arranged to meet her at the ferry slip, where the trains were carried on barges back and forth to San Francisco. Jane, the child of the cleaners, a white-blond silent little girl, came along with us when we left. We promised to have her back in an hour. We stopped at the market and had the butcher slice us half a pound of paper-thin salami, and we bought a tiny jar of mayonnaise and a loaf of Wonder Bread, which I wanted so badly that my eyes filled with tears when my mother at first said no. Wonder was the living bread to me and we never had it at our house. We had wheat breads, black breads, dead breads. We took our food and a tiny wooden ice cream spoon for the mayonnaise over to the ferry slip across the railroad yard and sat down in a semicircle. Boats steamed and sailed past, off to Oakland, off to San Francisco, off to Angel Island, and the gulls cried and cars passed behind us, and the world smelled of diesel oil, old wood and rust, and cold salty water full of seaweed and crabs and cool clean fish. It smelled of the coast and of trains.

Finally we heard Natalie limping toward us, clodhopper nun-shoes on the rough splintering planks, and my mother turned her face up to be kissed and held her arm out rigidly for Natalie to hold on to as she lowered herself to the ground. She massaged her hip for a minute, and then turned to pat and tousle Jane's hair. Jane looked like a ghostly deep-sea fish. I was not sure why we had brought her along.

My mother began making salami sandwiches, using her legs as a table. Natalie sat hyperventilating, chewing gum like a waitress in a diner, making cat's cradles with a huge rubberband. It had been three weeks since she quit smoking. Her stomach stuck out more every day. She was wearing plaid pedal pushers and a peach-colored beaded cardigan, lots of mascara, lots of foundation, lots of lipstick, and a peach stretch headband, as though her big black hairdo were capable of any movement whatsoever, as if it had to be restrained.

"Is it getting any easier?" my mother asked.

Natalie shook her head and snapped her gum. In the first two weeks she would come over and sit down on our couch and then flop around all over the place, then suddenly hug herself around the stomach and moan. Then she would raise her head and stare at the ceiling in a way that made you think she might start keening. One day I picked up the phone in the kitchen right as my mother answered it in her bedroom and Natalie bleated: "MY HEAD IS FULL OF BEES!"

My mother invited her over for dinner that night and Natalie stopped crying. She and my parents were sitting around before dinner having martinis when Natalie started crying again. I brought her a box of Kleenex, and she pulled me into her lap and cried into my hair and kept saying, "I hate this, I hate this, I hate this." My mother went outside to smoke. When she returned Natalie was sniffling bravely. I was in her lap and my father was holding her hand. "Darling," he said. "It is the hardest thing on earth; the hardest thing I've ever done. And you're under some terrible pressure right now, it may not be the right time to quit."

"But it isn't good for the baby."

"Maybe it's better than being tortured like this. The whole thing is wearing you down."

"I feel a little bit better."

"Good, but play it by ear. Marie smoked through both her pregnancies and the babies turned out fine. I mean, you're holding Exhibit B."

"Are you trying to get me to smoke?"

"No, no! I'm just saying that if it turns out to be too hard, and you end up having to smoke, we'll love and admire you every bit as much as we do now."

She looked at him with her big drag-queen eyes. "Really?"

He looked at her gently, rueful and wise, and then shook his head. "No," he said and she laughed.

My mother gave Jane and me the remaining loaf of bread and asked us to disappear for a while, so we went to the edge of the apron and threw the bread to screaming gulls, sometimes sailing slices out sideways, like you skip pebbles, sometimes wadding slices up into ping-pong–sized balls and hurtling them at the gulls. I looked back at the two women talking. I thought of Natalie and Ed together. I did not know what went on when people made love and did not believe for a second what Casey had told me, but imagined Ed and Natalie hugging each other in bed, hugging, kissing, nicely, and then giving one another more aggressive snuffily hugs, and then God knows what. My mother was being careful not to smoke in front of Natalie. They were hanging their heads, sitting only a few inches from one another. Through it all Jane did not say a word, only chucked her pieces of bread into the water. She was beginning to unnerve me. I considered pushing her off the apron and into the bay.

My mother wouldn't tell me what she and Natalie had been talking about until after we dropped Jane off at the cleaners. Hot starchy air billowed out when we opened the door. It was one of my favorite smells. It smelled like Peg and Ed's house. They didn't ever have enough money to take their clothes to the cleaners and so Peg always had the ironing board out and it smelled so good as she ironed her family's clothes, of hot laundered clothing and starch and warmth. Ed spent too much money when he was drinking. He lived beyond their means, spending money he didn't have on people he didn't like. And so the family did without.

"What we talked about," said my mother, after we left the cleaners, "was a plan I have. Ed and Peg desperately need some money, and we hardly have any to give them. But I'm going to go to Carmel and talk to Peg's parents. They have all kinds of dough, but they've never liked Ed. The only time they ever helped them out was the first year after Lynnie was born."

"How come they don't like Ed?"

"Because he knocked Peg up, remember?"

"Why do you have to go?"

"I've been praying and praying, darling. And what I know is that they need money, so that Peg and Lynnie—and Ed if he wants—can get some therapy. So that Lynnie will have someone she can talk to about this. Peg and Ed are too far into their own pain to help her right now. But therapy costs an arm and a leg, and Peg can't ask her parents for help right now. Now they're punishing her for leaving Ed, even though they've encouraged her to do so."

"You said there was going to be a solution. But things are getting worse and worse."

"Oh, darling. I don't know, maybe my going to Carmel is part of the solution. But you know me, honey, I'm the one who thinks God can do anything—your father says I'm going to end up on Market Street wearing a sandwich board for Jesus. And I really do believe He's working all of this out for us. It's just that I don't know exactly *how*, or when. But He's a foxy one, babe."

We were sitting in the car and I started to cry.

"But we were going to go shopping," I wept. "You said."

"But darling, listen."

"You *said*."

"I know I did. But we'll have to put it off a week."

I kept crying.

"Sweetheart, you hate shopping with me, remember? I don't do it well, and it makes us both crazy. It's like daddy says: By the time we're done, we're like two people slumped against the mission walls, dribbling, half passed out, and someone has stolen our shoes."

"What about my school clothes?"

"Natalie'll take you shopping. Remember how much fun you two had when you went that time?"

"Can't I go with you to Carmel?"

"No."

"Does Casey get to go?"

"No. Not even Daddy gets to go. I have to go alone."

I remember that Casey and I were both hanging out in the study with our father on the morning my mother left. Dad was going over a manuscript with a blue pencil. Casey was absently cutting strips of paper on our father's big green gridded paper cutter because he liked the whistling sound the sharp blade made when you brought it down fast. I was staring out the study window—filled with anxieties, troubled, dreamy, somehow numb and wired all at once. My mother had been on the phone with Peg all morning. Ed didn't want her to go. Peg was afraid it would make things even worse but was willing to let my mother give it a try. My mother kept saying that God could do anything. Like old black Willie at church always said, You just had to axe.

"God hasn't brought you this far to drop you on your head now," she said. "Wait and see. There is a way. You wait and see."

In the second-story study the trees grew so close to the windows that it looked and felt like a huge tent had been draped over the entire house, a tent of redwood, pine, and ivy. I heard the rustle of my father's pencil on his manuscript, crossing something out; the rush of the paper cutter's blade as Casey cut another sheet of paper into strips; my mother on the phone with Natalie, down the hall. I went outside down those long Mayan steps and found a place in the ivy behind some trees where no one would ever find me, and called for the kitty in a whisper.

When Peg's mother called that night, I didn't even know who she was, but her voice was quavery as she asked to speak to my father.

"May I please tell him who's calling?" I asked.

"This is Mrs. Schindler," she said. "Peg's mother"—and I knew right then that my mother was in serious trouble. I was crying by the time I got my father, who was in the kitchen making dinner, and he talked on the phone for a minute and his face went white and blank, and I raced up the stairs to get Casey, who looked furious when he saw how terrified I was. And then we were in the kitchen staring up at our father. He was having a drink of whiskey and wiping furiously at his eyes.

"Your mother's hurt," he said, "but she's alive."

Casey was saying, "What! What!" and then he slugged my father in the hipbone and hurt his hand and started crying, and my father said to Mrs. Schindler, "Wait a sec." Then he put the phone down and grabbed Casey by the wrists. "She's going to be okay," he said. "She's going to be okay."

"Is it bad, is it bad?"

"Yes." He was nodding, and then he pulled me into him and pulled Casey in against us, and it was like silent sirens going off in the room. "She got hit, really hard, outside the Schindlers'," he said, "by a man," and I started to weep really hard because in my mind I saw some man attack my mother, hit her in the face, bruising her, blackening her eyes like the women who showed up at our house in the middle of the night.

"She's been hit by a car," he said.

Mrs. Schindler said that a lot of things were broken in my mother, but the doctors said she would live. Mr. Schindler was at the hospital with my mother. Mrs. Schindler had tried to get ahold of Peg and Ed, but they were not home.

"I'll be there in a couple of hours," my father said. "Maybe three. I need to take care of the kids. I'll meet you at the hospital. No," he said after listening a minute, "I think it would be better if I left them here with Natalie. A friend of ours."

Natalie arrived with her boys and two sleeping bags half an hour later, while my father packed his overnight bag, called the hospital, wrote down the phone numbers of the Schindlers and the hospital for Natalie, had another drink, and packed the bottle.

"She left the Schindlers'," he told us. "I don't know how things went, but she left and she was crossing the street, and that's it. She got hit, that's all I know. But I'll call you as soon as I've seen her. And Nat, you need to call Ed and Peg. Mrs. Schindler is going back to the hospital. You know the number? Okay, good." He gave everyone, including the twins, hugs and kisses. Casey and I walked him out to the car.

Natalie had found a package of my mother's cigarettes by the time we got inside, and was smoking on the couch. We set up camp in the living room, with sleeping bags and pillows, sandwiches, cookies, mugs of cocoa, wine and cigarettes for Natalie. We lay in stiff positions watching television. Somehow time passed. It became night. Every so often Natalie went into the kitchen and tried to get ahold of Peg and Ed. My father called and told Natalie that my mother was lucky to be alive and would live. There had been a lot of internal bleeding and a lot of bones were broken and her right leg was smashed, but all in all she had gotten off easy. The Schindlers felt responsible. They had not been able to reach Peg either but spoke of her kindly. Then he talked to Casey for a while, and then he talked to me. He was on the verge of tears the whole time. He said it was from relief. I felt that the world was coming to an end.

I fell asleep with my head in Natalie's lap. The boys were all stretched out on the floor in their sleeping bags watching a western. When I woke up I was in my parents' bed. It was pitch dark and absolutely silent and I was deeply confused. Then I got out of bed and went downstairs. The clock in the living room said twelve-thirty. Casey and Dan were asleep, but the other twin, Matt, was lying on his stomach propped up on his elbows inside the sleeping bag, still watching TV, the volume so low I could hardly hear it. Natalie was lying on the couch smoking. She sat up when she saw me, and I lay down again with my head in her lap and she stroked me as she would a cat. I heard the trees outside the window blowing in the wind. Matt turned around to look at me and I couldn't blink. After a while I started drifting off to sleep. Natalie's pants smelled clean and crisp, like hospital sheets.

I came to at some point and heard Natalie on the phone in the kitchen. I looked down at Matt and saw that he was asleep. The television was on with no sound. I got up and went into the kitchen.

Natalie was standing with her back against the refrigerator. She had the phone pressed between her ear and shoulder, and held her arms out to me. I started crying again and walked over to burrow against her. She was talking to Peg. "If you and Ed want to go down tomorrow, why don't you leave Lynnie here with us? Nanny would love it, I know. Right now it's all boys. Anyway, I'll call you as soon as Robbie calls me." She didn't say anything for a while and I had the impression that Peg wasn't speaking either. "Jesus," said Natalie. She stayed on the line with Peg awhile longer, although she didn't say very much. I put my arms up for Natalie to lift me, which she did, although she hadn't picked me up for over a year. I held on to her neck and wrapped my legs around her waist. Then I remembered she was pregnant. I held on, draped over her left shoulder. I heard the wind in the trees, the owl. She held the phone to her right ear and helped hold me up with her left forearm and she rocked with me from side to side.

By the time my mother got out of the hospital three months later, Natalie's belly was as round and as full as the moon. Peg and she were speaking, not exactly like friends but more like divorced people who are starting to get along. They spoke once a week at the suggestion of Peg's therapist. It was sort of a miracle. Maybe my mother had been right all along. I began to almost believe in God again, in whatever it was that my mother believed in, even though I didn't quite know what that was; like when Mrs. Einstein said she really didn't understand the theory of relativity, but that Albert did, and she knew he could be trusted. Natalie came over nearly every day and went for a short limping walk with my mother. We were back in our own home. Our dandelion patches were of two minds, half bright yellow flowers, half round heads of white down that the wind could scatter to seed. The leaves of our blackberry bushes were yellowing, some of them scarlet as poison oak and most still green, and at first you'd see only little dead berries and burrs but then a sprig with fat red berries. Ivy grew through the blackberry bushes; wrentits sang. I mourned when my mother left for walks with Natalie. At home Jeffey and I hung around her like a bad smell, and she needed to get away from us, even just to take a walk with Natalie, only a block or so at first, hobbling, hitching along.

Four

THE FORESTS all through Northern California were on fire. You could smell the smoke in the air night and day. My parents had gone away for the weekend, down to Monterey. My father had been back only six weeks, after having left us for a month. It was 1963, the year the fifties ended, and the fathers in our town were leaving. They walked out the front door, following the piper in his suit of many colors. No one knew who or what this new piper was, who played the tune that called our fathers away, but one of the fathers had *Playboy*s hidden in his study. His daughter and I found them one day and stared speechless at the huge pale-pink breasts and hairless pubes. It was our collective great fear, that our fathers would leave us, start new families with younger and prettier children; we had seen it happen before. There had only been two children in first grade whose fathers had left, whose new wives had babies. In third grade there were seven children whose fathers had left, and by the end of the fourth grade, the year President Kennedy was killed, nine out of twenty-three kids had fathers who were gone.

So it was no wonder the rest of us had become a little skittish.

Once when I was spending the weekend with Peg and Ed and Lynnie, Ed was very late for dinner and Lynnie and I became convinced he had left for good. We had helped Peg bake and frost a chocolate cake from scratch, to surprise Ed when he came home from his new salesman job, but he didn't come home. Lynnie grew even quieter than usual. We set the table, but Peg told us to go play for another half hour, so we went into the basement and stripped and did our Dance of the Veils, our nudie revue. While we were getting dressed, Lynnie whispered in my ear, "I don't think he's coming back."

"You don't?"

She shook her head solemnly.

I didn't think he was coming back, either. We went up and into the kitchen, where Peg was crying at the stove, cooking three hamburger patties.

"It's after seven," she said, without turning to look at us. "He said he'd be home around five." Lynnie and I stood behind her, studying the floor. "Where could he be? He's drinking. Well, I hope he never comes home," she said, and then we heard a car horn honk, and the three of us tore outside. Peg was holding her spatula like a flyswatter, like she was going to rush up to Ed's car and swat him, but then she put it down and walked to their old slate-blue Nash Rambler and opened Ed's door. He got out. He was a little bit drunk, and held a brown paper bag by its neck. Lynnie and I stood thirty or so feet away; Lynnie was happy and scared, chewing on the feet of a blue-haired troll doll she had grabbed on the way out, staring sort of stupidly at Ed.

"I thought you had left us," Peg finally cried, but Ed raised his bag in triumph.

"I've been hunting!" he bellowed.

The bag was full of black-red plums. Peg became silent, and weird, and powerful. I don't remember if they fought or if we ate any of the plums, but I can still see the sky, how pink and purple fog was rolling in, low, flooding the hills.

We went inside. I didn't feel very well, and called home to see if my father had left us. He hadn't. I sat down to eat—there was a fabulous red jello salad with fruit cocktail in it—but my stomach was upset, and then I heard a headache coming on. My vision shifted and somehow before the laser was turned on I got my Uncle Ed to drive me home. He was very quiet, very gentle in the car. My father carried me up to my bed, tucked me in, turned off the light, told my brother to turn off his radio, and helped my mother care for me until I fell asleep.

My father left us several months later. I don't remember much about it. My mother spent that month smoking, praying, putting in a garden with flowers and vegetables in alphabetized rows: asparagus, broccoli, cauliflower, daisies. And the local tennis ladies all took to introducing me to each other by my full name. They trolled the boardwalk shops doing their errands and looking for one another, to compare morning round-robin scores and gossip. Their legs were very brown but when they took off their shoes their feet from the ankles down were as white as the balls we used back then. "Robbie and Marie's daughter?" they would say after giving my full name, all to jog their friend's mind—Robbie, *you know*, who just left Marie? And you could see Ah So! in the other woman's eyes. So Robbie's left Marie! "Hel*lo*," they would say, and I would reply, Hello Mrs. Collins, Hello Mrs. Mueller, Hello Mrs. Brown, and paw the splintery dark planks of the boardwalk, and stare through the slats into the black space below, shift my eyes to see the little pom-poms at the back of their socks, just above the shoe line, where their tans began. Some who also swam had tan feet too, and all of them painted their toes, and all of them shaved and oiled their legs, their still young legs.

Mady White's mother was a tennis lady, with one whole drawer full of pom-pom socks, and she had luncheons at her house all the time. She played in the Wednesday morning round robin, with the truly terrible players, the beginners who would always be beginners. Sometimes a temporary beginner would join the Wednesday morning group, and even her beginner's game would go downhill after a few minutes chasing down unintentional lobs, unintentional drop shots, and balls suddenly coming at her at fifty miles an hour while she stood at the net, with her back turned, about to walk back to the baseline.

Every Wednesday afternoon after school there would still be four or five women in their little tennis skirts and dresses sitting in the patio at Mady White's house, sipping white wine, talking about the children who caused trouble at school, the men who were said to be having affairs, the problems of women not present. Once I heard them talking about Natalie: one of them was wondering why her ex-husband hadn't cut off her alimony when she had her illegitimate baby. They did not seem to know that the baby's father was Uncle Ed; but in any case they didn't like Natalie's looks, her tight white pedal pushers, dyed black beehive hair, big black drag-queen eyes.

Mady and I nibbled on their leftovers out in the kitchen. They had had Chicken Rice Roger. Everyone was eating Chicken Rice Roger that year. My mother only made it once; it didn't turn out right. Essentially all you had to do was pour a can of chicken stock over uncooked rice and chicken breasts, and bake it until the rice was done. But something went wrong, who knows what, and it didn't turn out at all, and my father had been in a tense, end-of-the-month mood to begin with.

"Darling?" he asked politely. "What the *hell* is this?"

"Chicken Rice Roger. Just eat it, darling."

He squinted at her, as if she was out of focus, but she was watching Casey pour himself a glass of milk.

I watched him rev up for an ethical consultation. "Excuse me," he said, "darling? Excuse me a second, just, just wait, darling, now—Chicken Rice Roger? CHICKEN RICE ROGER?" My mother was looking at me, grimly helpful; I was pouring myself some milk now, and my stomach was buckling with shame. Casey was scowling at his plate of food, and my father began to drum his fingers on the table, saying, "Darling, excuse me—excuse me—did you say—did I hear right, Chicken? Rice? ROGER?"

And Casey shouted, "Good *Dog*, Carl," with exasperated sarcasm, and my father laughed so abruptly that he snorted red wine out of his nose, and Casey and I started laughing, and then my mother started laughing, put her face down into her hands and was crying, too.

When she stayed like that for a while, I decided she was praying. She used to say she was a walking prayer, always saying, Help me, help me, help me, or thank you, thank you, thank you. She looked over at Casey and snickered, nicely, and Casey poked shyly at his food, and then my mother got up, the relief on her face unmistakable. She looked like she did when our heater would finally make the house stop being so cold, and she walked off to the kitchen. I breathed a long deep sigh. Casey and Dad started talking about Casey's Little League practice. I listened for the sound of my mother, of her lighter in the kitchen, snapping. Then it must have caught, because the sound stopped and after a minute I could smell her cigarette smoke.

Casey and I stayed with Natalie and her twins and the baby that weekend mom and dad went down to Monterey, when the forests all through Northern California were on fire. Lucy, the baby, hardly ever cried. She was nearly a year old. Uncle Ed and Aunt Peg, alone and together, had run into Natalie and the baby several times in town, and they both just admired the baby with as much grace as they could muster, before saying good-bye and moving on.

I got to sleep with Natalie that weekend. The baby slept in a crib in the corner of the room, and she cried to be fed only once. I listened to Natalie nurse her in the near dark, to the sucking sounds. The baby looked a lot like the baby pictures of Lynnie. She was a great baby. She made Natalie very happy, and the twins essentially treated her like a new pet.

Natalie was changing her diapers when I woke up that morning, and I watched for a while and then wandered the house wishing Casey would wake up. The light from the morning sun poured slanting into the living room; a long trapezoid of sunlight fell on the reddish blond hardwood floors. Where the sun fell on white—typing paper, an opened book on the ledge below the window—shallow bowls of white fire glowed.

The twins had pictures of their father all over the walls of their bedrooms, pictures of him in his navy uniform, pictures of him and Natalie holding them as babies. Theirs had been the first father to leave. He was very handsome. They stayed with him every other weekend, in San Francisco, out in the avenues. Gabriel McCall, everyone called him Gabe; he called Natalie Nat when he called, every other Friday.

Natalie took us to the rec center after lunch on Saturday. She kept making us put on more Sea and Ski, every time we came out of the water to sprawl on the bleachers, salty, steaming, and she gave us lots of dimes for frozen candy bars. The last fifteen minutes of every hour was Adult Swim—all the kids had to get out of the water and all the adults got in and swam laps. In one quadrant, the right corner of the deep end, the water ballet team got to practice, even though they weren't adults. They were teenage girls, all the way up to eighteen, floating on their backs, kicking prettily, heads out of the water—all that turquoise blue water barely rippling—dipping underwater into blurs below the surface, in their brightly petaled caps and tank suits. God, I thought they were the most beautiful things on earth. Next to us on the bleachers were the Burton children, five of them watching their mother swim laps. She was fat with another baby, swimming in a maternity tennis dress, crossed rackets over one breast, huge ruffled panties, and on her head she wore a purple petaled swim cap. Her husband had left her when my father left my mother, but her husband hadn't come back.

Husbands were leaving, leaving; every couple of months it seemed another one was gone. Their children would be at the rec center with extra pocket money for snacks. They would have money to burn and would buy us things so that we would hang out with them. I cultivated friendships with them, like I cultivated friendships with the Catholic children, for tuna-noodle casserole or English muffin pizzas on Fridays. You could cry at the club because everyone's eyes were red from the chlorine anyway, except for the women who didn't let their heads go underwater. There was too much bleach in the water, it turned green when we peed, and our blond hair turned green—even though we wore caps, it turned the palest light green, pale seaweed green, like mermaids. The Burton children wore white plastic sunglasses, all five of them, from the ten-year-old girl Teresa, to the two-year-old boy they called Jimbo, and they solemnly watched their mother swim, and in their white plastic glasses they might have been in the desert, watching the A-bomb tests.

I wanted to go to my mother's church the next morning, but Natalie said it was too beautiful out, so we made Casey and the twins two chopped-olive sandwiches each, which we put in my father's worn-out drab-green canvas knapsack. The boys collected two dozen crab apples from the tree out back, tiny, sour, wild. They piled into the car with their rods and tackle boxes, and we drove them first to the bait shop and then to the trailhead, which led to the lake where they went to fish for bass. They turned to wave fifty feet from the car, then disappeared around a curve in the road.

I felt rashy with jealousy watching Natalie cradle and talk to Lucy, who gurgled and smiled all blond and rosy with wonderfully squinty blue eyes, while I lumped around, teary, skittish, dark, homesick. Natalie must have noticed, because she arranged for a girl to come baby-sit in the afternoon when it was time for Lucy's nap.

We walked into town and did a couple of errands and then went to Nellie's coffee shop for hot fudge sundaes, even though Natalie was on a diet. Nellie brought me a silver blender canister with some-body's leftover strawberry milkshake and poured it into a Coke glass for me, and I sat there eating and drinking while the women talked. Both of them had beehive hairdos. Nellie said so-and-so's husband had left, and Natalie's mouth dropped open. I didn't know the fam-ily. They didn't have any kids in Casey's grade or mine.

Natalie was stroking my head while I ate.

"Nanny's father says they're leaving because of the Chicken Rice Roger. That that's why they're all jumping ship."

Nellie beamed at me as I ate. Adults, if they weren't your parents, always beamed at you when you ate, beamed like you were success-fully using a fork for the first time. She fished around in her apron pocket for her pack of cigarettes, took one out, lit it. "*That*'ll put a little meat on your bones; skinniest little girl in town. Don't you worry, I was skinny too, no boobies at all either."

"I'm only eight," I implored.

Nellie had huge bosoms and also dark blue squiggly lines near the tip of her nose, scars from a car accident. The first time my father came in here, and Nellie had brought him a cheeseburger and a glass of ice water, my father dipped his handkerchief into his water and wiped at the tip of her nose. She just stood there. He thought it was ink.

After leaving the coffee shop, Natalie and I went to the railroad yard and sat Indian-style in the dirt beside the tracks in the shadow of a kingly black locomotive. There were two hobos asleep underneath the caboose, safely asleep since the trains didn't run on Sundays. They were not much older than my father. I had peered down to stare in at them until Natalie dragged me away. I made a joke. I said to Natalie that maybe they had left their homes because of the Chicken Rice Roger. Natalie kissed the air in my direction. And then we sat down by the old locomotive.

The hot summer air was filled with smells of steel and dirt and grease and diesel, with the coconut lotion Natalie always wore and with smoke from the forest fires up north. Natalie fished a bottle of nail polish out of her purse, shook it for a long time, then began to paint her nails red.

"I thought maybe you wanted to talk about when your father left." I looked up at the black locomotive and shrugged. She didn't see me. "Hmmm?" she asked, and I looked over my shoulder at the mountain, shrugging again.

She looked over at me, squinting one eye. "You have the right to remain silent," she said. "Anything you say can—and will—be used against you." She raised her hand close to her mouth, to inspect and then blow on her nails. Then she began to paint the nails of her other hand.

"Will you paint mine too?"

"Yep." She looked up. "I never knew a father who loved his kids as much as yours does. He really loves you guys."

"*I* know."

"But his head is always filled with stories he's working on, and right in the middle the Sears bill'll come, and he's already teaching too many hours. I think he starts to feel defeated. And then he shuts down; I've seen him. Here darling, give me your hand now. I'll do yours, and then I'll give myself a second coat." I put my hand, palm down, on her knee. She dipped the brush back into the nail polish. So many birds were in the railroad yard, singing. "I've seen him shut her out, you know, your mother. And she's so sensitive, it's like she's a recovering burn victim, all pink skin. Not always. But he goes into his head and then, it's like: 'I didn't mean to hurt you, didn't notice you were there.' " She bent forward to blow my nails dry.

Walking home on dirt roads, we came around a bend in the green-red-brown redwood shade and saw Earl Palabinkeses and his daughter Tina standing on the footbridge, dropping pebbles into the water below. Tina was one month older than I, and had a relatively mild form of Down's syndrome. The creek was very low—it looked like water had leaked into the creek bed, settling around slate gray rocks, like someone was going to have to mop it up. Moss covered the redwood trunks, and ivy laced itself, quite far sometimes, up the trunk. From up on the bridge where we joined Tina and her father, the water skeeters sitting on the creek looked like the glass snow-flakes we hung on our tree at Christmas. Unseen wind chimes played. Birds were singing everywhere. There were ferns and bamboo plants growing amongst the ivy, on the banks of the creek, all that ivy, and yellow leaves, and copper leaves, reddish leaves, pine needles turning brown, but mostly green, green leaves. Earl—Mr. Palabinkeses, we called him—was tennis-pro handsome, blond and shaggy and tan. My father didn't like him much, didn't like his long impenetrable silences. I remember him telling my mother, "I always find myself feeling like a parody of myself around Earl." I didn't know what he meant at the time. At one of our fishhouse punch Christmas parties I discovered Earl hugging Carrie Conners' mother in the downstairs bathroom. This sort of thing happened routinely at our house, since we had frequent parties and I had trouble sleeping; I was always coming upon people who weren't couples, hugging in corners of the house, in the bathrooms, in the garden. It utterly confused me, like being in a dream where you get up close to the person you think is your friend, but it turns out they have blind dog eyes, or gills.

The Palabinkeses family moved on to our street when I was in first grade. Gussy Palabinkeses and Casey were in third together, Mrs. Bosomhead's class. (Mrs. Bosomhead's real name was Mrs. Buvvenhead.) Casey stayed the night at Gussy's house a number of times, and so my mother invited Mrs. Palabinkeses to tea.

Mady White and I had been banished from the Whites' house because Mrs. White was hosting a tennis luncheon for the Wednesday morning round-robin group. She was making tomato aspic and Chicken Rice Roger. So we hiked over to my house and found my mother tearing around the living room picking things up, stuffing them under her arms to dump en masse on her bedroom floor, carrying stacks of library books to my father's study.

"Mrs. Palabinkeses is coming to tea with her daughter," she said. "Give me a hand, my darlings. Now you know the little girl is retarded, and you know not to stare, right? Right? Okay darlings." She was wearing a huge ratty white T-shirt of my father's, worn almost to transparency—you could see the diamond pattern on the cups of her bra—sky-blue gingham pedal pushers, and bleached-out blue deck shoes with the laces undone and holes cut out so her big toes could breathe, so her hangnails wouldn't hurt. "Help me vacuum, lambchop. Mady, you don't have to." But Mady wanted to. After I vacuumed the cat hair off the couches and our oriental rug and the dark hardwood floor that framed the rug, Mady took the attachment off the nozzle and with grim efficiency began to vacuum up all the daddy longlegs that lived in our corners—that had always lived in our corners. I gasped, frozen with shame. Zzzzoooop! Zzzzooop! She went from corner to corner, sucking up all the spiders; I saw them all imprisoned in the vacuum bag, covered with dirt and dust bunnies, flailing, suffocating. I wanted to cry out, "We don't do that here!" but suddenly it seemed the right thing to do, the clean and civilized thing to do, the Catholic thing to do. And so I stood there miserably and let Mady vacuum up my family's spiders, Mady with her old-lady vinegar mouth, grim as if she were from the Health Department and we had just been busted.

Though my mother suggested that maybe Mady and I should go into town—"Here," she said, "I'll give you each a quarter"—and even though candy was our life, the getting of it our vocation, we chose to stay. We promised to be good. We promised not to stare. We promised to act perfectly normal in every way, to pretend that we were quite used to seeing little retarded girls. And then there was a knock at the door.

My mother crossed herself, dusted off her hands, and went into the hall to open the door.

Tina Palabinkeses was in a stroller on our doorstep with her mother. She was my age but looked about four, dressed in a little yellow sunsuit that tied over each shoulder. She had long blond pigtails, tied with lavender grosgrain, black lashes on slanted blue eyes, a long scratch on her wide flat skull, enormous bottom lids, and her head and eyes were sort of lolling around. She was smiling. I was so intent on not staring that I gazed up and around at the ceiling as though I were at the planetarium, and Mady bared her teeth like Alfalfa.

This was the first time we met Tina—in her little plaid Keds and purple grosgrain ribbons—but after that I saw her all the time. Over the years she grew stronger and stronger. Her mother spent hundreds of hours with her in the pool at the rec center, where she learned to swim the crawl. Her hair turned that pale mermaid green, light see-through green. I saw her at every little-league baseball game I ever went to, because our brothers were on the same team and their father, Gus and Tina's father, was the coach. Mueller's Hardware Store sponsored them, Mueller's was in felt letters on the back of their jerseys. I sat on the bench next to Tina a hundred times, both of us in car coats, chewing bubblegum, cheering on the boys, who almost always lost. Casey loved baseball with a desperate passion, but he ran funny, gangly and slow. He could never hit the ball past the bases, but they let him play right field, where he couldn't do much harm unless a left-handed hitter was up to bat, in which case Carrie Conners' brother Steve moved over to the right, as did the left fielder, Mighty Owen Turner. Casey never complained, never even cringed; he just wanted to play, wanted to be part of the team. He was in love with the game. Mr. Palabinkeses hardly paid any attention to Casey at all, but Casey didn't seem to mind.

The adults shared thermoses filled with hot coffee and booze, pacing between the bleachers and the dugout at the junior high school field, rubbing their upper arms to get the circulation going, huddling together against the night cold. Carrie and Steve Conners' mother was always at the games, wearing little ski clothes, parkas and black stretch pants with stirrups. She was a great mother: she would let you eat jello straight from the box when you came to play at her house. You could pour it into your palm and lick it up languidly, lick up the juice it left when it was all dissolved; you didn't have to steal the box from the pantry and eat it on the sly, like you did at other kids' houses, like you did at our house.

When I found her and Earl Palabinkeses in our bathroom, I rather blithely assumed—after the inital shock—that I was just having a nightmare.

Mrs. Palabinkeses was German and had the most enormous breasts. She was a tennis lady whose dresses had to be specially made. When she hit a forehand she needed to bend down toward the net and swing with her arm level with her face; had she lowered her arm and swung like a normal person, her stroke would have been halted by her breasts a third of the way into the swing—they would have stopped her arm, like door jambs. On her backhand, she had to fold her arms across her body with her elbow crooked-in against her nose, well above the ledge of her bosom. She had a scar on the side of her nose, from her stint with the Wednesday morning round-robin group—one of her opponents tore hell-bent up to the net to execute an overhead smash, but lost her grip on the racket. Mrs. Palabinkeses, also at the net, had not had time to shield her face. Whenever the ladies of the Wednesday morning round-robin group sashayed proudly around town, up and down the boardwalk, in their tennis dresses, pom-pom socks, and sneakers, you could see the terrible gashes and bruises on their shinbones from when it had been their turn to serve.

In any case, that day when we saw Earl and Tina on the footbridge, Earl had just left his wife. Natalie and I did not find this out for several more hours, but when we got to the bridge and said our hellos, Earl began to look agitated. He finally confided that he had to be somewhere for business right then, it had entirely slipped his mind, and he asked us would we mind if Tina played with us for a couple of hours, until Mrs. Palabinkeses got home? He didn't mention that she had run screaming from the house an hour before, but I still didn't believe his story. I thought he was going to see Mrs. Conners, that they would rush into each other's arms and hug.

So the three of us walked into town. Tina didn't talk very much. Natalie bought us each a tiny fishing tackle bag full of gold-nugget bubblegum, little yellow lumps of gum in muslin drawstring bags. She bought herself a can of beer. We set off, across the lazy railroad yard, along a narrow path that ran like a zipper up the hill where we sledded on cardboard all summer and fall, through the woods, on the old fire road, and finally to a field where two old goats grazed. I had known them all my life, their names were Pedro and Easter. They let us pet them, butting us gently, and Tina squealed and peeped. The goats' owners came out, but I had known them all my life too—the lady was the town librarian, her husband worked in the railroad yard—and they waved when they saw it was me, before going back inside. They were both in their fifties, which seemed very old to me.

Tina stood there petting the goats, peeping away. Natalie stood sipping her beer, gazing around at the field, the low golden hills beyond, the wide groves of cypress here and there. Then Tina started asking for her father. She had a very strong but plaintive voice. Natalie explained that he had gone to work and that in a while we would go back to her house, and her mother would be there. Tina didn't say anything or cry, just ate her fool's-gold gum. Natalie and I took her over to the concrete pool, four feet by four feet by four feet, which a spring filled with freezing mountain-cold water, and it was filled with frogs, and completely surrounded by blackberry bushes, with water skeeters and dragonflies skittering across the dark green water. The frogs sang and talked, burping, and the three of us climbed on to the edge of the pool, Natalie holding Tina, while we rolled our pants up to our knees, and gingerly, squealing, gasping, lowered our legs into the icy water, sitting with our butts on the wet ledge, still gasping. We could hear the goats and of course the frogs, could turn around and pluck a perfect berry, or if you liked, a green-and-red one. Natalie kept handing Tina perfect fat purple berries. We got juice all over our clothes. There were a lot of spiderwebs in the blackberry bushes and an occasional spider, some small and black or brown, some as gaudy as painted Mexican masks. And some of the berries were overly ripe, beginning to mold, and left a gray spidery aftertaste in your mouth.

Tina was such a nice person. When we took her home, her mother's eyes were red and swollen and she had been drinking. She told Natalie, and Natalie told me later, that Earl had packed his bags and left. This is what the fathers did, packed their bags and left and lived in motels until they found apartments, and showed up to get the kids for weekends, or alternate weekends, and Wednesday nights. If you were there when they drove away on Wednesday nights, you could see that they looked sick, like they were on the verge of throwing up or like they had seen a ghost.

When my father left us that one month and we didn't see him at all, Casey hardly spoke to me. I got migraines. My mother lost ten pounds and smoked so much you couldn't stand the smell of the house. It smelled like a barbecue pit. My father smelled like a strong-smelling man, like a clean goat, like the ocean and a garden. I liked the smell of cow flops, of gasoline and skunk, and I loved the smells in the bathroom when my father emerged, when he had been on the toilet after showering and shaving, all those smells together. My mother said he would come back, and that we must pray in faith. You had to believe that God could hear and answer your prayers, because that's what He loves. He loves faith. Otherwise, my mother said, it's like that story, those people out in the Midwest, during the decade's worst drought, when an entire congregation goes trooping outside to pray for rain, and only one small boy brings an umbrella.

When my father came back, we all ended up in their bedroom, my mother on the bed crying, Casey sitting slouched over beside her, with our cat in his lap, petting him like nothing big had happened, and I helped my father put his things away. I remember him handing me his cedar shoe box, and how I opened the lid of the box to inhale the smells of the shoe polish, the Kiwi black, the Kiwi brown, the little round tins with the kiwi bird in the middle, the sharp rich smell of turpentine and candlewax, and how I cradled the box on the way to its place in his closet, on the floor pushed into the corner beside his two pairs of wing tips, one pair black, one pair brown.

Five

MY BROTHER TURNED thirteen in the late winter of 1966, the year Ronald Reagan ran against Pat Brown for governor of California. We called him Reegen, as did all the old lefties with whom my parents gathered to fight the great good fights. Uncle Ed called him Ronnie the Rat. The people who came to our house to stuff envelopes for Brown, over cocktails or wine, with Monk or Mozart on the hi-fi, were by now as often as not divorced, or their marriages so flagrantly on the rocks that the next time we hosted a gathering, one of them wouldn't be there. Soon there were more women than men stuffing envelopes, women about to turn forty. The piper had lured their husbands away, to other towns and cities, sometimes other countries—Mexico, for instance, where Earl Palabinkeses ran off to with Owen Turner's mother. The fathers and the occasional mother came back to visit their first batches of children when they could, weekends or summers or birthdays.

Every year for my brother's birthday, the world outside our house was as green as a rain forest, Ireland green, and then all the trees burst into blossom, apple, plum, fig, and looked like they were covered with snow. Everything was upside down that year my brother turned thirteen, when the piper came back for the children—Ronald Reagan on the ballot, all the fathers leaving home, what looked like snow on all our trees, and after a bad wind blew, big round tree snowflakes on our porch, on our steps made of rock, on the leaves of ivy, on the webs that spanned the leaves.

Natalie had moved away a year before, down to San Diego with her three kids. It was too hard on Ed for their baby to be growing up in town and to hardly get to see her, and it was too hard on Peg for Ed to feel bad about it all the time. So Natalie moved. It was very painful. Ed somehow managed to stay sober. Peg went to a group called Al-Anon and overate. Lynnie went to ballet class every day and looked like she was starving to death, but seemed very happy all the time. My father had stopped smoking, as had many other people in our circle, but my mother still smoked three packs a day. Mostly now she smoked in the downstairs bathroom, where Jeffey's box was. The room smelled awful, of cat box and smoke, and everyone but my mother and Jeffey had stopped using it long ago. Uncle Ed called it the Lion's Den.

My mother spent inordinate amounts of time talking to Jeffey, and working on politics, stuffing envelopes, taking petitions door-to-door, or setting up tables down on the boardwalk, passing out leaflets, registering Democrats, collecting money for her causes. I still went to church with her every Sunday, although I was no longer sure I believed in God. I just loved the singing. My mother said that maybe I would believe again one day, that she had gone through long periods of disbelief too, and then would again come to feel Jesus hanging around her, like a stray cat or dog, and she would finally with exasperation quit resisting, throw up her hands, and tell him he could come in for the night.

We no longer had a dog. We had gone through two since our lovely but gassy basset hound had been put to sleep. I still remember

Natalie loading him into the back of her station wagon—he was over fifteen by then—and as I watched from the window, I saw that Natalie's face was animated with the strain of everything put together: his destination, his gas, his weight. My father and brother had gone fishing, and my mother hid in the Lion's Den.

The two dogs since had manifested all of my father's compulsions, my mother's depressions, Casey's impending hormonal prostration, my migraines and my fears. On two occasions, perfectly adorable puppies entered into our care, into our seemingly healthy home, and our lives revolved around their puppyhood for about a week. We put my father's travel alarm clock into the little nests we made for them in cardboard boxes, and we fed the puppies puppy mush, and lied and cried to get out of cleaning up their puppy shit, and fought about whose turn it was to walk them, fuming and jerking them along when it was our turn on a busy homework night. They were always getting out, and we'd have to spend hours tracking them down. They would be friendly with us—after all, they were on the family plan, too—but with everyone else who came to our door, they were skittish, neurotic, snarling, little canine portraits of Dorian Gray, embodying our angst and bad nerves. Neither of them lasted very long. One got run over, one ran away.

Peg and Ed, who, unlike my parents, yelled at each other and cried, had two great dogs during my childhood, a black lab that Lynnie had named Sarah-Jane and a German boxer mix named Max Schmeling. One of my earliest memories is of Christmas at Peg and Ed's, when Lynnie was three and I was four and Sarah-Jane was still a puppy. My father was sitting cross-legged in front of the fire, with me sitting in the triangle of his legs. He had his chin on the top of my head, except when he reached for his glass of red wine. Everyone else was around the piano, singing carols, while Peg played, and Ed got drunker and cried about how happy he was, about what a lucky, lucky man he was, and the puppy was asleep within petting distance of where my father and I sat. My father reached for a piece of salami on the antipasto plate on the hearth, and before folding it into quarters to lower into my mouth, he held it to the sleeping puppy's nose. Sarah-Jane flinched, sniffed, flinched again, whinnied softly. My father squinted at her. "The smell went up into her dreams," he said.

When my brother turned thirteen, he stopped going out with us for dinner. He didn't even go to Ed and Peg's anymore. A few times in the beginning Dad made him come along, and on the way spoke to both of us strictly, about how civilized, how helpful, how polite, we were all going to be. "*Just*," he said, "so we're all on the same sheet of music."

But once there, someone would end up mad at someone else, half the time over a game of ping-pong, and Casey would end up brooding in the living room, alone.

We didn't sing anymore after dinner at Ed and Peg's—no more hobo songs, no more train songs, no more ballads. Ed had bought himself a ping-pong table with all the money he was saving by not buying booze. Lynnie and I always wandered off right after dinner, while everyone digested, and hit the ball softly back and forth, trying just to keep it in play for as long as possible, solemn but full of joy. But then the others would arrive and break all rules of order and protocol by making us give them the paddles, without them having to make a challenge and work their way into the game. Peg and my father never played, but did the dishes together. Ed and Casey would begin, rallying way too long. Casey would give Ed a run for his money, but try too hard and almost always lose, and he'd hit the table with his paddle and make a dent, and my mother would cry out sharply at him. He would stalk off and brood in the living room, and my mother would take up his paddle, meek and self-effacing, while Ed crossed himself and looked to the ceiling for help.

My mother was normally so dignified, always at least slightly depressed, often so close to tears that my father had taken to calling her

the Lesley Gore of Christendom; but at the ping-pong table she became an ice princess—whippet thin, steely, compelled, ruthless.
She had grown up around male cousins who taught her tennis and
then ping-pong, and she was good. Years later, Casey and I told her
how scared we had been as children, to face her across the ping-pong
table. "Really," Casey said. "You were like some mad cross between
G. Gordon Liddy and the entire Chinese Olympic ping-pong
team," and my mother just stared at him, as though he had just spoken to her in Bengali. She always beat Uncle Ed, who would then
hand one of us his paddle. "Now, go easy on her, cookie," he would
tell my mother, and she would start off hitting us balls we could return, and then the plates of her face would shift, almost impercep-
tibly, and the balls would come at us like bullets. I could get some of
them back, but Lynnie would end up cringing, shielding her face
with her hands, holding them close and poised for defense like a
boxer.

For his thirteenth birthday, Casey declined the usual family
party, where our mother would cook you exactly what you wanted,
and Peg and Ed and Lynnie and Grandma Bette, and several of our
best family friends, the ones we called uncle and aunt, and a couple
of commies thrown in for flavor would come bearing gifts, and after
dinner we would all sing songs. For his thirteenth birthday, Casey
got to take the ferry into San Francisco with some friends. Some of
them were girls. They spent the day in the city, doing God knows
what, returning at ten that night, red-eyed and tired and smelling
dirty. My father and I picked them up in our Volkswagen bus at the
ferry slip. They seemed very mature to me. No one said very much in
the car, just perfunctory answers to my father's questions about what
they had done the whole time. They said they had hung out in
Golden Gate Park. There had been a concert. The two girls had frail
wreaths of tiny daisies in their long blond hair. I was mute with jealousy. When I see thirteen-year-olds now, I see how terribly, how poi-

gnantly young they are, but they seemed almost grown-up to me at eleven. Most of the girls had gotten breasts and wore bras, and they all went to dances and didn't play with balls at lunch and recess anymore. Now, at lunch and recess, they did what adults did: hung out in small groups and talked, or went behind the shed at the far end of the playing field, where adults sold hot dogs during Little League games, and smoked. We all looked up to them. We still played at lunch—four-square, two-square, tetherball, softball workups—and while we waited for our turns we watched the big kids hanging out. They ignored us, the girls with their breasts and bell-bottom pants, the boys with their shaggy Beatles hair and pegged blue jeans; so blasé and world-wise, you almost expected the boys to be smoking pipes.

As it turns out, they were smoking pipes, pipes of marijuana. This was the smoke, hanging in the air as clear as the notes of a lute, that called my brother away.

Because my brother now shunned my parents, I went with them everywhere, as if I could be two children in one. When my father went over the mountain to drink beer and cheap red wine with his writer friends in someone's garden, up on the hillside above the ocean, I went along. When my mother went into the city to register voters, or into town to shop, or over to Peg's to garden, I went along. When my father and mother went to stand outside the gates of San Quentin, in silent vigil with other lefties, dad's writer friends, mom's old black Christian friends from church, at dawn on the morning someone was going to die in the gas chamber, I went along.

And I went along because I was so profoundly lonely. Mady and I weren't very good friends anymore. I was no longer allowed at her home, the wonderful house with the huge magnolia tree we used to climb, which bloomed with rosy purple flowers. It was Grandma Bette's fault, more or less. My parents had been down in the South, my father covering the civil rights marches for a magazine, and Bette was baby-sitting and one day decided to take Mady and me to see *Whatever Happened to Baby Jane?* She thought it was about dolls. Further, she thought eleven-year-old girls still loved dolls, and I don't really understand why Mady and I agreed to go, or why they sold us tickets, or how we got past the movie posters that must surely have indicated it was a horror movie. All I remember is that Bette stayed with us until the young Baby Jane does her macabre tap dance, and then she slipped out to go flirt with the homo owner of the bakery across the street, flirt him into giving her some sticky buns; and when she returned, it was to find me watching the end of the scene where Bette Davis serves up the dead bird, with Mady in the bathroom throwing up popcorn and chocolate stars. Grandma Bette asked us both not to mention this to our parents, but Mady was in the back of our car, lying on the floor, staring up with glazed unseeing eyes; and when she got home, she not only mentioned it to her parents, but proceeded to have a full-blown, if brief, nervous breakdown, in the aftermath of which she was forbidden to play with me anymore.

But we did play together for a while, together with another friend named Donna, at Donna's house, which was up the hill from where I sat on the steps of the church, not far from Mighty Owen Turner's. Mostly we lay around Donna's pink bedroom, chewing gum and leafing through old issues of *Seventeen* magazine that her cousin Punkin had given her. Oh to live in a family with a cousin named Punkin. But one terrible afternoon when I returned from the bathroom, Mady and Donna were smiling too nicely at me. I smiled back, but Mady now was studying my hair, with glee. It was nearly white, curly as a black person's. I kept smiling. I had in fact begun to beam.

"Want to go into town?" I asked.

"In a sec," said Mady. "Sit down a sec, I want to try something."

It did not occur to me to say no. I sat where Mady pointed, at Donna's vanity table, and stared into my lap, as Mady parceled off a small section of my hair and began to braid it. I knew what she was doing. The black girls at my mother's church braided their hair without needing rubber bands to secure it, and that was what Mady was doing, proving that my hair was just like a black's. And it was, and they held, the little braids she made, while I sat there, frozen, smiling, and she hummed a little tune, like a hunter hums while strapping his kill to the top of the car.

For a while after that, I didn't play with anyone except my cousin Lynnie. I called her Punkin. But she was practicing her ballet most of the time, and I spent many afternoons endlessly throwing a baseball against the wall next to the garage door, hurtling fastball grounders to myself, to catch with the mitt my brother no longer used.

I had played with other girls besides Mady and Donna since our falling-out, and even spent the night at their houses, but more often than not I wound up alone, abandoned. For instance, right around my brother's thirteenth birthday, when the blossoms were just appearing on the trees in our yard, the plum and apple and fig trees, I had been banished from the house without having done anything wrong. It was very confusing. My father came into my bedroom quite early one Saturday morning, sat on my bed and woke me. He smelled terrible, hung-over. It was not yet truly light. "Nanny darling," he said. "Wake up. Your mother and I are having a bit of a bad morning. Why don't you get yourself ready to go, and I'll drive you into town." I had heard them, earlier, when the dawn was just breaking, purple and golden and rose, my mother angry and crying, my father begging for sleep. They had left for a cocktail party the night before at six and were still not home by midnight when I finally fell asleep.

My father told me and Casey he would drop us off anywhere we wanted to go, but we couldn't come home until the afternoon.

"I have nowhere to go," I wailed. Casey, tired and angry, asked to be dropped off at the boardwalk, none of whose shops would be open for another two hours, and I got out with him.

"Hey, kids," my father said. Casey was just about to slam the door. "I'm sorry." All three of us shrugged at the same time. "Here," he said and handed us a five-dollar bill.

It was a bright misty morning and only a few cars were on the road. Casey and I walked through town. It was very quiet. During the week now, all over town, machines arrived in the early morning to level the hills, to fill in the swamps, to tear down the building in the railroad yard which housed the turntable where men used to fix the locomotives. All over town the sounds rang out, of backhoes, pneumatic drills, chainsaws, and dump trucks rumbling past like tanks, carrying away the wood and concrete of old buildings, old trees, load after load of soil. Buildings went up overnight, houses, apartment buildings, little boutiques.

"I'm going to go to Owen's," he said. We were walking up the hill to the little white church.

"Can I come with you?"

"No. It wouldn't be cool. Can't you go to Mady's?"

"No."

"Go see Peg and Ed then. Here, you can have the money."

I didn't say anything for a while. I honestly couldn't think of anywhere to go. Casey knocked softly on the side of my head like you knock on a door, and when I looked over, he handed me the five-dollar bill.

"Take it." His hair was dirty and getting long, but he was very kind that morning. He was like our father. All the fruit trees we passed were in bloom.

I sat on the steps of the little white church for a long time that morning, after Casey dropped me off and kept going, toward Owen's house. Behind me, above the green hill, were long curvy clouds, gray, like dolphins. Across the water San Francisco was hidden in fog, and way down at the foot of the town, the masts of the boats in the harbor sprang out of the blue-green bay like quills, and there were cars on the road in town, now, people with places to go.

Partly out of this new round of loneliness I started to go to church with my mother again. She was so grateful for the company. She missed Natalie dreadfully, as did I, and we both missed and were afraid of Casey. My father made scrambled eggs and black bread toast for us every Sunday and then settled in with the *New York Times*, while my mother and I put on our dresses and good sweaters, and walked together to the quonset-hut church in the housing development where the town's really poor people, mostly black people, lived.

The quonset hut was huge, with a cross on top of the roof, and a pulpit that had once been a podium at the junior high school I now attended. Instead of pews, there were folding chairs in a semicircle, split down the middle by an aisle. There were four stained-glass pictures suspended from the rafters—one of a lamb, one of bread and wine, one of grapes and stalks of wheat, one of a black hand grasping a white hand. There was a huge batik scroll against one wall, in purples and blues and red, with the words from the Book of Micah, where the strong nations shall beat their swords into plowshares, and their spears into pruning hooks, and shall study war no more.

There were usually forty or so people at worship, mostly black and Mexican, with half a dozen whites; the choir of seven black women and one elderly white man sang us several songs and led us in the singing of the hymns throughout the service. They wore their own clothes, not choir robes. They were paid to clean houses by the women in town, who gave them clothes for their children, and sometimes clothes for themselves, and shirts with frayed collars and cuffs for their men, who mostly didn't come to church. In town you saw the men drive by in old cars, but not at the market and not in the stores; the men, in their frayed Brooks Brothers shirts and scuffed brown shoes, you saw them at the liquor store. I always stood behind my father while he talked to them. I could hardly understand them: they said "fillins" for feelings, "jury" for jewelry.

My mother and I sat down by ourselves and listened to the choir sing spirituals, while the church filled up. Everyone had processed hair. The room first smelled of the hundred burning candles, and as it filled up with people it smelled of starch, it smelled like Peg's laundry room when she starched and ironed their clothes. Then it smelled of booze and oil, urine, grime. Wino John had come. He was standing next to me, in white cords caked with oil and dirt, a red-and-black checked lumberjack's jacket dotted with burrs and dried grass. He was scanning the faces of the congregation in disbelief, as if all these people were camped on his living room floor. He looked down at me. Through the beard and the leathery skin, the red-rimmed blue hawk eyes, the small straight nose that was always running, you could see that he must have been an incredibly handsome child. Casey had dressed up as a hobo two Halloweens ago, with a beard and a lot of burnt cork, ragged patched pants, smudged lipstick ringing his eyes, and the resemblance was chilling. He and John might have been father and son.

"Hi, Nanny," he said.

I whispered back hello, scared because my mother didn't like him, nice because my father did. There were hardly any trains running now, but a couple of men still lived in the railroad yard. I saw him there often, after school and during the summers, hanging around, often alone, drinking white port or stout malt liquor. My father said that John was very smart. They were the same age. At his own home, in the railroad yard, he was pleasant, polite in a backwoods way; but at church he was, as often as not, a royal pain in the neck. He hissed at things no one else could see and spent entire sermons writing angrily, intently, on dirty scraps of paper or on the mimeographed program. The breast pocket of his lumberjack's jacket was always filled with paper scraps and pencil stubs and used envelopes into which he stuffed his missives. He then delivered them to our pastor, James, while James was still preaching. James, tall, handsome, black, and radical, had tried for a while to control John's interruptions, but had long ago given up; now he reached for John's envelopes as if this were a normal part of the worship service, which in a way I suppose it was. Then John would shuffle, sniffling and hawking, back to his chair. The other parishioners didn't react to him at all, didn't seem to notice him except to say hello after the service. They seemed to believe, all but my mother, that maybe he was crazy, always half-drunk, stinking to high heaven, always a pain in the neck, but also surely a child of God.

He was the one person I ever knew of, besides Richard Nixon, that my mother just simply hated.

James came over to our house one afternoon to talk about it with her. The three of us sat out on the porch and drank pink lemonade, while James pretended not to be afraid of our cat. He didn't take his eyes off Jeffey for very long, and I had the feeling that if Jeffey had jumped up into his lap, James would have screamed. I remember him telling us that day that when there was someone in his life he didn't like, he thought of the story in the old rabbinical texts, of Moses leading his people out of Egypt, and how after the Red Sea parted, the Hebrews turned to watch the walls of water covering the pharaoh's horsemen and chariots. And Moses turned to God to thank Him, but saw that God was crying.

"Why are you crying, oh Lord?" he asked, and God answered, "Those were my children, too."

"That doesn't sound rabbinical, James," my mother said.

James didn't answer right away. He had his eyes trained on Jeffey, who was sitting on the white rattan table, looking at James lazily, evilly, snaking his head up and around from time to time to peer into James' lap, as if maybe James had a mouse hidden there.

James said, "All I know is, John is my brother. The Lord is his shepherd, too; and you know He told us, feed my sheep."

This was what the sermon was on, that Sunday, when I smelled John before I saw him, standing beside me, sniffling.

James read us the passage in the gospel where the risen Christ keeps asking Simon Peter if he loves him, and each time Peter says yes, yes, Jesus says Feed my sheep. Then James looked up from the battered black Bible, smiled, looked around at us, sighed.

"I didn't start my sermon till last night," he said. "But right after dinner I rolled back my sleeves and started working real hard, real fast. I'd been thinking about it all week, but hadn't put a word to paper. It was about this passage, about how we must take care of everyone, those less fortunate than we who have so much. It was about the God-shaped hole the early Christians said we have, which can only be filled by God, and how He fills us by giving us the desire to love and serve His children. It was about how we must learn to love our enemies, like Martin is doing in Selma today, loving the racist. Loving the racist. It was about how we must feed the hungry, shelter the homeless, nurse the sick—when all of a sudden my phone rings.

"It was close to eleven o'clock, and the caller was a drunk or crazy young woman, calling from San Rafael, who needed a place to sleep, and she hadn't eaten all day, and she didn't have a penny left, had borrowed the dime to call me. 'How did you find my name?' I asked, in total exasperation.

" 'I went through the phone book,' she said. 'Looking for a reverend.'

" 'But my name begins with an R,' I implored.

" 'I just found it, Rev.'

"And I knew," he continued, "that if I stopped, and went to where she was calling me from, and found her a place for the night, and took her there, I wouldn't be able to finish my sermon. And I knew that if I didn't, I couldn't *deliver* my sermon. So I looked up at the ceiling, shook my head slowly, and said, 'God? You're messing with me.'"

All the while the old black man in the corner said, "Uh huh, oh yeah, ay-men."

And James found her a bed in a county facility for the night, but consequently the sermon was going to be a little shorter than usual, and we were all laughing, everyone was happy, and the pianist spontaneously started playing "Freely, Freely," and everyone started singing, even though James wasn't done preaching. While singing I suddenly sniffed the air, like a dog, turning my head while I tracked the scent, of lovely BO, soap, and old red wine. My father was several steps away. I gasped, and my mother turned to me and then saw my father, and the next thing I knew we were walking outside.

I could hear the people singing as I trailed along behind my parents, like a dog. "Freely, freely, ye have received; freely, freely, give." I couldn't hear what my father was telling my mother, but Casey was in trouble. He had, as it turned out, been busted.

Casey was in the backseat of the Volkswagen bus glowering, unkempt. He and Owen Turner had been caught driving around in Owen's father's car, which was blue inside with marijuana smoke when the cops pulled them over.

"Hi, Casey," I said.

He was looking out the window and didn't say anything.

He was in so much trouble. My body, my whole being was red with shame. This wasn't like when we got yelled at and were sent to our rooms without any dinner. This was big time.

"You're grounded for a month," my father said grimly, before sliding the bus's back door shut, slamming it closed, as if we'd never get out again.

"It's not fair," Casey muttered.

"What'd you say?" my father roared, whipping the door open.

"Nothing."

"*What did you say?*"

"I said, it's not fair, it's too—"

"*Fair?* Fair? Fair would be that you'd both be dead."

My father drove us home. No one spoke. I kept stealing glances at Casey, wishing he would just look back at me for a second. He smelled terrible. I remembered all the times he had been in disgrace before, sent to his room without supper, and how I would sneak him cookies and oranges; but this time was different.

Things never seemed the same again, after Casey got busted. There was often an edge in the air, like bad weather was coming. We weren't as close to Peg and Ed, or at any rate we didn't see them as often. One night, while Casey was still grounded, the three of us went over there for dinner, and I walked in feeling safe and happy. I threw myself against Aunt Peg in the kitchen, and she scooped me halfway up, and kissed the back of my neck over and over, then my cheeks, and said how good I smelled, how clean, and how pretty I had become. She was really quite fat by now, her skin soft and pink and smelling like Ivory soap, but she wasn't one of those fat women who let their cleavage show, like Wendy Harper's mother, with her big clammy moist bosom, always pulling me into her until I was blind and couldn't breathe.

Peg was frying chicken, and was going to serve Lynnie and me in the TV room, so we could watch *The Wizard of Oz* while we ate. It was heaven. Uncle Ed ended up bringing us our food, on TV trays, kissing us both, staying to watch the first fifteen minutes with us.

Lynnie took the deep-fried skin off her chicken, and folded it up neatly so that it still fit on her plate, and when Uncle Ed left, I chided her gently, feeling very big sisterly, saying she needed to eat the skin, she was getting too thin.

"Please, Punkin," I said, "please eat the skin," but she just smiled nicely at me for a moment, and turned back to the set. "Punkin, I'm serious," I said, and this time, she smiled tightly without looking at me, and dropped the chicken skin to the ground, where Sarah-Jane gobbled it up. Then we heard my father's angry voice and turned straining toward the source.

As it turned out, he and Aunt Peg had had a small fight. He happened to mention that he'd had a chest X-ray, because the doctor was worried about his cough. He had smoked Pall Malls for twenty years, and even though he'd quit a couple of years ago, he still coughed too much. But the X-ray looked fine, the doctor said, there was nothing to worry about. At which point in my father's story, Peg began pooh-poohing the reliability of X-rays.

My father had jumped on her, and Peg had begun to cry, and Ed had gotten mad at my father for making her cry, and as usual my mother had managed to soothe everyone and turn the talk back to something else. But we left the second the movie ended.

My father began to rant in the car; he was having a postmortem ethical consultation.

"Darling, why would someone *do* that?" he demanded.

"Peg just doesn't think sometimes."

"Doesn't think? Dear God. Sometimes she's got all the tact of a cow flop—by the time she was done, she had implied that for all the information an X-ray showed, the doctor might just as well stare at your chest, with you just not wearing your T-shirt."

My mother burst out laughing.

"Well, darling, didn't she? Didn't she imply that? People are grave dancers, doll. I notice this whenever I have a book come out. If

I get a bad review, friends and acquaintances groan for me, commiserating, but on the inside, they feel a tickle of pleasure—a tickle of relief, that it's you, and not them."

"Robbie, you're ranting."

"I am not ranting, Marie. I know that this makes them feel very bad, this grave-dancing business. And I know that it isn't their fault. I know they were raised by screwed-up, frightened parents, and that they in effect got shitty owner's manuals. But still. That goddamn Peg."

I knew my mother was thinking religious thoughts, about not judging, or about trying to remember what Peg had been through.

"What do you mean?" I said, "Shitty owner's manuals?" But we were pulling up outside our house, and all the lights were off.

"That goddamn kid had better not have left—he's grounded another month if he has," and the moment we stepped inside, my father called out, "Casey, Casey?" and from his darkened bedroom, Casey called back, "Yeah?"

My parents looked at each other, and then my mother walked down the hallway toward Casey's room. My father stood there, kneading his face, and then went downstairs. I just stayed where I was. I could hardly hear what my mother was saying, but then Casey said something sharp to her. I heard her slap him. Then I heard my father downstairs dropping ice into a glass. My hearing felt muffled, as if I had just gotten off a plane. I opened my mouth and pulled my earlobes down, until my ears popped.

I kept trying to cheer up my father. I had seen him cry over Casey, after one dinner where Casey had been unable to respond to much of anything. My father had gone to his study and closed the door and when I walked past with our dinner dishes, I peeped in and saw him at his desk, hunched over, eyes closed, like in the Gospel of John when Jesus cried.

So I took him for walks on the weekends, along the shore or the salt marsh, or up on the mountain. We ambled along with our hands in our pockets; he wore a porkpie hat.

"Can you keep a secret?" he asked one morning late that spring. Of course I could keep a secret. I was the keeper of the family secrets. My mother told me everything and then made me promise not to tell anyone. My brother bragged about some of his exploits to me and swore me to secrecy. If he and I were alone at the house, I would look up from the deck to find him hanging from his bedroom window, smoking a joint, and I would say hi, and after a pause he would say hello back, and I never once told my parents. I had been raised not to tattle. Uncle Ed asked me once if Natalie ever called, and I told him the truth, that yes, she did, that her little girl wore glasses and Natalie had a beau, and I didn't tell my mother that Ed had asked.

"Yes, I can," I told my father.

"Your mother wants to send Casey to a psychiatrist."

"Huh."

We walked along. We were between the two bridges on the salt marsh and the tide was pouring in. It rushed and flowed around the small dunes covered with bright green moss, these dunes in a huge ring framed by thick bullrushes. The top of every dune was flattened and bright green, and as we stood on the one bridge watching, it came to resemble a massive turtle's back.

"Your mother can't accept that Casey is just growing up. You know her, she likes to fix us all. Like her blood is epoxy. That's why she married me, doll! Boy, was I a real fixer-upper. And most of the people who come to your mother want to be fixed, and so we let her fix us. But Casey doesn't even think he's broken. And maybe he isn't, and anyway Nanny, don't you think to be human *is* to be broken?"

I nodded knowingly.

"It even has its own beauty, to be broken," he said.

"There's an avocet," I said.

"That a girl . . . It's very hard for your mother right now. I try to remember what Joyce said—that God keeps a gentle eye on the world, while He pares His nails. And I'm trying to sit back a bit, keep a gentle eye on Casey, while I pare my nails. But sometimes he pushes us too hard, and it's very hard on your mother. There's a story machine in her head, cranking out scenes of disaster. I guess we all have it, to some degree, but she worries too much—well, so do I. I don't know what the difference is." Now we were facing the crystalline mirror-flat bay, green as jade today. The eucalyptus groves on the hills to the left were perfectly reflected, the leaves a flatter gray-green than the water. Most of the surface of the bay was taken up by three hills across the way, and near the shore an egret stood in its own reflection, snowy white feathers on black pencil legs on the snowy white image of itself, in all that green, green water.

"I said to her, 'Darling? Ed and I were talking at the beach the other day. About how Natalie had to move away, how Peg cried all the time for a while, sure that Ed would leave her—' And how probably Ed won't see that daughter much until she's all the way grown—and how terrible, how utterly unreal it feels to him. How huge the ramifications were, of two lonely friends going to bed—your mother and brother both lost their best friends, Peg nearly lost her mind—but Natalie sure loves that baby of hers . . . And anyway, sweetheart, the point I was making . . ."

"You were saying something to Mom."

"That's right, I said to her what Ed said to me, which was why do we make it all seem like a crisis, over and over again? Why do we worry it all to death, like dogs with socks or chew-toys? 'Look at it this way,' he said to me. 'In a hundred years? —All new people.'"

Sometimes the three of us would be watching television after dinner, not very often, and Casey would come in and stand in the doorway watching us watch television, as though he had found us playing with our coloring books. He'd then get caught up in whatever we were watching, and sit down next to one of us. When he sat down next to my mother or me, we would be so happy we could hardly concentrate on the show. When he sat down next to my father, Dad would reach over and begin to scratch Casey's jutting shoulder blades, without taking his eyes off the set, then every so often glance over surreptitiously, see the long hair, the red eyes, and sigh.

I remember us watching a show on wildebeests one Sunday night. Casey was sitting next to my mother in the loveseat. He was watching the set, and she was watching his hair grow, really studying his head, as if there were a map on it and she was trying to track a route cross-country. Finally he turned to her, and said, "Do you mind?" The narrator was saying that some wildebeests got a fatal illness called Turning Disease. They caught it from bugs. It affected their equilibrium in such a way that all they could do was to turn and turn and turn, walking in small circles, some of them faster than others, but mostly quite slowly, for days or weeks, alone. The lucky ones got killed by hyenas, instead of turning themselves to death.

"Dear God," said my father.

"Wino John had it today in church. The whole time James was preaching. He actually had it, didn't he, Nan? Turning and turning, with the weight of the world on his shoulders. I kept thinking that at least it was keeping him quiet."

"I'll tell you what I see in this," said Casey. "Mr. Allen has been reading us Thoreau. I see this as about men leading lives of quiet desperation, just turning and turning, sick till they die."

My father nodded sagely.

"There's hope for him yet," he said to my mother after Casey had left the room.

Things were sort of peaceful for a few days, until Saturday when my father and I were walking through the railroad yard on our way into town. There were hardly any trains left. There were new houses on the hills above the railroad yard and everywhere you looked. Suddenly my father put his right arm out to stop me—as if we were in the car and he was braking out of the blue—and then he jammed his hands in his pockets and stalked over to where wino John and three of my brother's friends stood, on the ground in the shade of a loco- motive, each with a bottle of stout malt liquor. Wino John raised his bottle in salute. Mighty Owen Turner's mouth fell open, and he put his bottle of stout behind his back, while Allan and Greg Schneider both looked extremely hopeful—as if my father had brought them some nice snacks to go with their beer.

My father glared at John, who smirked, and Owen studied the ground at his feet, and the Schneider boys beamed like idiots. "If you're buying these boys beer, I'm going to knock you into tomor- row," said my father.

"Not me," said John. "I'm eighty-sixed anyway. I can't even buy these days for me. They brought *me* this stout."

"We just had an extra," said Owen.

"Wasn't that thoughtful of you," said my father.

I don't recall what happened next, except that we made it home in record time, my father muttering the entire way, and me seemingly forgotten behind him. Casey was actually home doing homework, and my father tried to pick a fight with my mother at the entrance to Casey's room, and then lit into Casey for having friends who drank stout malt liquor with the winos.

"You go away somewhere," he said to me, and I threw up my hands and stalked into my room. He followed me. "Go to the rec center, go into town—I really don't care where you go, but go."

"Darling," my mother said from the distance. "Leave her alone." My father and I glared at each other, and after a minute he left the room. I went and sat in a corner with my knees pulled up to my chest, crying. My heart was full of sympathy for Casey. Right then I hated my father too. I saw myself standing up to him, hands on my hips, sneering. You can't tell us who our friends can be—I would say—I have two friends who *none* of the parents and none of the teachers like, and they're totally cool, and they are the only people these days who have been totally nice to me.

I wasn't terribly close to the two girls, whom none of the parents liked, but I wanted to be close to them, wanted to be like them. Not so long before, just before the trees went into bloom, I got to spend the night in the harbor aboard a Columbia 29 with them. Their names were Gigi and Pru. Gigi's father owned the sailboat. They were twelve, and defiant enough for Casey and his friends to hang out with them a little bit at school. Gigi had three older sisters and got away with murder, got to wear eyeliner to school in seventh grade. She wrote with her oldest sister's beautiful neat script, none of the letters slanting at all. When we became friends, in sixth grade, I tried to emulate this, having always gotten C's in handwriting before, and now I wrote half in my sloppy boyish way and half in Gigi's style. Actually, I didn't know what my own handwriting looked like anymore, but I started getting B's.

Pru's mother was thin and dark and slutty and mean and single, and Pru's older sister was thin and dark and gorgeous and slutty and mean, and had taught chubby Pru all the fast-girl ways of style and fashion. How to wear eyeliner, shave her legs, how to bleach her hair with peroxide, how to wear underpants over her pantyhose to keep them from bagging. She and Gigi both wore pantyhose to school, with Keds. They both wore bras and had already had boyfriends. They were allies with the truly bad girls, the really cheap slutty ones, the ones whose fathers were gone or were western white-trash drunks. They went with older boys, high school boys, sometimes— even at twelve with college boys. They shoplifted clothes, smoked cigarettes, drank rum and Cokes. They were everything I wanted to be. A few times they had let me hang out with them, and we went to Pru's and listened to 45's and smoked. Her mother was never home.

We had to bring in our own food because Pru's mother kept a padlock on the refrigerator.

The air in the harbor that night on the boat smelled of sea and algae, smelled of sex, and we smoked a few cigarettes we had bought from the machine at the rec center. We went inside and, the next thing I knew, Gigi and I were trying to pull off Pru's skin-tight pegged light-blue jeans. We were pantsing Pru. She was lying on the bunk in the back and we were all thrilled and aroused, pulling at her jeans; she was writhing, pretending to resist, and we were giggling, hot and red. She was wearing red lace bikini underpants, and I could see pubic hairs poking out on the sides, and I could hardly stand it, pulling and pulling at her tight pants, feeling her soft warm skin against my hands. This was so much better than sitting around Donna's house, reading her cousin Punkin's magazines. I was half out of my mind. When we had wrestled her jeans down to her ankles, we stopped, and we let her pull them back on, sheepish now, all three of us. The sailboats rubbing against the sides of the berths groaned, and harbor seals barked, and even from inside we could smell the sea, the algae, the fish, and then we were pantsing Gigi. We rolled around on her, tugging at her pants, laughing, squirming girl bodies, me gaping bug-eyed and delirious at her white lacy bikini panties, dark hair showing underneath. I felt such tightening in me, down there, a tightening in my crotch, like someone was turning the crank on a winch. And in my head I felt like a wide-eyed gasping puppy who is being tossed its first few balls. But then we were done with Gigi, and no one thought to pants me. I felt a little bit like crying, rejected, but then we all went outside and sat in the cockpit, and flushed, underneath the starry diamond sky, we smoked.

We slept in separate sleeping bags that night. They slept in the bunks, I slept on the floor between them, like a dog. We talked all

night. I was in my brother's sleeping bag, which was lined in red
felt, printed with hunters and deer, pointers and ducks. When we finally stopped talking, I lay in the dark, silently kissing the back of
my hand. I practiced kissing a lot in those days. I kissed the mirror
in my bedroom, behind closed doors, and watched myself to see
what I would look like being kissed. I didn't think I would ever be
kissed. My mother said she hadn't thought she would ever be, either.
She said she had been the tallest girl in the state. I was the shortest,
skinniest, ugliest. When I kissed the mirror, I tilted my head to one
side, like I had seen in the movies, and moved my head toward the
mirror, fluttering my eyelashes. My parents did not know that I
kissed mirrors, as I wiped the mirror clean of my lip prints. The tip
of my nose always hit the glass first. It was warm against the glass,
and my lips were cool.

My mother did, though, notice how often I studied myself in
other mirrors. I heard her talking to my father about it, asking him
if he and she had been so narcissistic in their youth.

"I suppose so," he said. "She's right on schedule, baby. You must
have studied the mirror, too. And remember what Camus said, it
was Camus, I think—that Narcissus was transfixed by his own reflection, because he was searching for something lovable in it."

Finally on that Saturday morning, when we had found Casey's
friends drinking with Wino John in the railroad yard, I couldn't
stand being inside any longer, and without saying anything to anyone, left the house and walked into town. I hated being seen alone. I
felt so forsaken that it was as if I had grown a huge tail, a dinosaur's
tail that dragged along behind me, for everyone in the streets and the
stores to see. Every time I saw someone I knew, my stomach buckled
and shame flooded me. Help me, help me, I prayed as I walked along
the boardwalk, clutching my stomach as though I had a bellyache,
and the next thing I knew, a girl was calling my name.

It was Pru. She was coming out of the record store with a new 45, looking like a Campbell's soup girl playing the town slut in the school play: white lipstick, black eyeliner, stockings with her Keds, a little white skirt, and a black poorboy shirt. She needed to peroxide her hair again. The roots were growing out black.

"Hey," I said.

"Hey."

"What are you doing?"

"Nothing much. What are you doing?"

"Nothing much."

Somehow—and it felt like a miracle at the time—I ended up at her house, sitting on the deck smoking Kents. I told her about wino John and Casey's friends, and how the winos bought the kids all the beer they wanted: the boys had to give the winos enough money for two of whatever they wanted, and the winos would take one out of the bag and leave the bag in a nearby trash can for the boys to collect when the winos were out of sight.

"How do you know that?"

"My brother told me. But I promised not to tell anyone."

"We better go into town. We're almost out of cigarettes; plus we better get some setting gel. Don't you ever wear lipstick?"

"Yeah, I wear white—but I just ran out."

"We'll get you some more at the dime store." So we walked along into town, bumping lightly into one another, and Pru told me her secret: that Gigi had ditched her a week ago.

"Gigi's a bitch," I said, my heart suddenly wild and warm.

Pru asked me if I could spend the night; we could set my hair. If you set kinky hair on rollers, it comes out soft and straight; oh, to have good hair. Oh, God. We made plans for the night, for the week.

"My sister'll get me beer if I ask. Do you drink very much?"

"Well," I said. "Pretty much."

The railroad yard was deserted except for the birds. We crossed it and walked into town, where, at the dime store, I bought my first tube of white lipstick. Then we headed toward the rec center, to buy cigarettes from the machine in the women's dressing room. We cut through an overgrown green and heathery field. A red-winged blackbird sang clear liquid notes from a patch of milky orange moss. I was in heaven, eleven years old; and all the blossoms on the fruit trees in my town had fallen like snow to the ground.

Six

IT LOOKED AS though Natalie and her daughter and new husband might come up for my twelfth birthday party, but I didn't let myself get my hopes up. They had intended to come up for the Fourth of July, because we hadn't seen her or Lucy in over a year, and we had never met the man she had rather suddenly married. Peg was willing to test whether the acceptance and forgiveness she felt toward the situation would hold if Natalie and Lucy were back in town, especially since Uncle Ed was so desperate to see his daughter again; and my mother was keen on letting all concerned see that God's grace, and time, were sufficient to heal such loss and confusion. By July first, however, Ed had shingles, I had had a cluster of migraines, my mother was laid up in bed with a sprained ankle and ringworm, Lucy had the runs, and Peg had the Turning Disease. So Natalie sent up a packet of photographs instead.

She looked exactly the same in the pictures as she had three years before, her beehive perhaps an inch shorter, those marvelous drag-queen eyes perhaps a little less crowded. Her new husband was a dead ringer for Fred MacMurray. In one picture he is holding Lucy out toward the camera as though she is an offering. She looked quite a lot like Lynnie, plain but angelic, with glasses and lots of red lipstick. The twins were nearly as tall as the new husband, very handsome, very straight. There was a picture of them in their wet suits, surfboards under their arms, posing in front of the San Diego tract house, looking cool. My mother first taped all the photographs to the refrigerator door, then took them all down in case Peg came over, and put them in the drawer of her night table.

One morning Peg stopped by after dropping Lynnie off at the ballet studio where Lynnie had a scholarship. She and my mother decided to walk into town for hot fudge sundaes at Nellie's coffee shop. I deigned to accompany them, since it was on my way to Pru's anyway. The leaves of the plum trees were purple black, and some of the trees were just beginning to turn—the few that do in this part of the world—flame colored. The backhoes and dump trucks and drills were all silent. We walked along the road above the railroad yard, where all working-class people still lived. In other parts of town and in the hills above us, rich people had moved in. People who had lived here all their lives had lost their views. Six months earlier the rec center had become a private swim and tennis club to which we did not belong. Pru and I still dropped by the women's dressing room there, to use the cigarette machine, but I was no longer allowed to go swimming. But before us that day when I walked with my mother and aunt into town, the mountain and sky still looked like a backdrop in a play, flat and brilliant, ethereal. The mountain was deep blackish green, the sky turquoise blue, and in front of this backdrop the low rolling hills—still without houses, but not for long—were absolutely pastoral.

My mother's limp had gotten less pronounced over the last couple of years, and since I no longer held her hand when we walked, walking with her no longer caused me to limp along too. Peg, though, always ended up limping. It caused me to wonder what it would be like when my mother and Natalie walked together, Natalie with her up-and-down limp, my mother's more of a scuttle, like India Schuyler's. India Schuyler was the person I most feared turning out like; only twenty-five years old but already crazier than a shithouse rat. She was a poet of local renown, who lived above the railroad yard with her husband, Alphonse, who was even older than my father. The two men were pretty good friends, and my father had once sent off a bunch of India's poems to his agent, but even so, India would cross the street to avoid having to say hello to him. She looked like I felt half the time. Uncle Ed called her Alphonse's pet ferret, and I always wanted to snick at her when we chanced to meet on the same side of the street. She was an unholy mirror. She wrote on her hands sometimes in ink to remember things by. I had peace signs drawn in ink all over the backs of my fingers that day. When we got to town, Peg nonchalantly took my hand, I began to scuttle too, filled with shame. I was nearly twelve and could not afford to be seen walking into town holding hands with a fat woman. I sighed and bowed my head and scuttled along, past the laundromat Pru's mother owned and ran.

At the northwest end of the railroad yard, in town, landscapers had just rototilled the earth, waiting for the train tracks to be pried up, as they soon would be. They had driven five huge posts into the ground, to form a ring like Stonehenge, and inside the circle four dogs were milling around, as if in a corral.

I told Pru that day about my Uncle Ed and Natalie. We were sitting on her deck, drinking Frescas, smoking cigarettes, painting our toenails pink. My transformation was nearly complete. I was no longer a skinny little kid who loved Jesus and Burl Ives, at home in the trees, on boulders, in streams, dressed in my brother's cast-off jeans. Now I was a skinny little kid in white lipstick, with my frizzy towheaded hair set every night so it looked like Doris Day and James Brown had mated. I wore the clothes Pru's dark slutty sister Alison handed down to me: pegged light-blue jeans and cotton ribbed shirts we called poorboys. When she gave me a poorboy, I would wait all day and night for it to be time for bed so I could get up the next morning and wear it to school.

I told Pru how Ed used to drink, how Peg had left him one summer, how Ed had gotten Natalie pregnant, how my mother had been nearly killed by a car, how Natalie had moved away, down south, and how we hadn't seen her for a while.

"How come?"

"Because it would have been too hard on my Aunt Peg."

"Aunt Peg's a big girl now."

I didn't say anything.

"Maybe Natalie has a new best friend."

Now she was making me crazy. "She doesn't have a new best friend. She and my mom talk on the phone all the time."

"I bet she does."

I wanted to smash my fist into Pru's face, and took a sip of Fresca to swallow the lump in my throat.

"My dad *never* saw me," she said.

"He didn't?" I reached casually for the pack of Marlboros, posed like a tennis lady, stretched out languidly in a chaise lounge, waiting for my toenail polish to dry. I put a cigarette in my mouth, shook one out for Pru, and we lit them off one match.

"Is he alive?" I asked.

"Probably."

"Is he Alison's father too?"

"No. Her dad owned the laundromat. He died."

"How'd he die?"

"He killed himself. With pills."

"How come?"

"I think he was depressed."

"Well, I guess," I said.

"My father was never married to my mother. I think he was married to someone else."

"Why do you think that?"

"Well, I know that, actually. My sister told me."

"Oh."

"My mother tried to have an abortion, down in Mexico, but it didn't take."

"How did you find out?"

"My mother told me."

"God, that's crazy, Pru."

"She was mad. I smashed up the refrigerator, trying to break the lock with a sledgehammer."

"Does your sister know who your dad was?"

"She says she doesn't. But there was this boy in town where we used to live, named Jonathan Curley. And in fourth grade he had a crush on me. We weren't allowed to play together, because his parents thought my mother was a slut. But one day we were waiting in the same line for four-square, and he was joking around, and he pulled his bottom lip down, like this." She pulled her bottom lip out and down, exposing her gums, and the two bottom teeth in front that crossed like fingers. She kept her lip pulled out, and looked off to one side and then to the other. "And his bottom teeth were exactly like mine."

"Did you ever do anything, or ask your mom or anything?"

She let go of her lip. "No. I always just wondered. His eyes were blue like mine, but squinty. His hair was dark and straight like mine. I didn't bleach it yet. I mean I was like ten years old or something."

I thought of Natalie and her new husband raising Lucy, letting her think the new husband was her father. "You'll love Natalie," I said. "And she'll love you. She's really neat. You have a lot in common." I said this because I wanted there to be someone who would love Pru. Probably all they had in common was that they were the last two people in California who were still ratting their hair.

My mother was kind but not exactly warm with Pru. She was, I suspect, bothered by Pru's chubby sexuality, and she didn't want me doing the things she suspected Pru of doing, doing the things her sister Alison was known to do with boys. I told her about how Pru's mother had told Pru about having tried to abort her; I told my mother so that she would be kinder to Pru, and she was. I heard her ranting at my father in bed the night that I told her.

He took me and Pru to the Fillmore not long after. It was our first time there. We got all dolled up, in our miniskirts, poorboys, black fishnet stockings, fringed moccasins, and white lipstick, and my father drove us into the city in our Volkswagen bus. I do not remember who we saw or what it was like being there. I only remember that Pru had her period, and that when we got over the Golden Gate Bridge she right away asked my father if he would pull over at a gas station. She had to go to the bathroom. I got out with her, and when we were done in the bathroom, we came back into the sunlight to find my father in a phone booth, talking away.

He was always dashing to pay phones, all of my youth. I never asked who he had to call. But we'd be at the zoo or the natural history museum, or heading into North Beach for dinner, or whatever, and he would announce that he had to make a call, and all three of us would wind up waiting impatiently for him, late for dinner, late for movies.

I thought for a while he was CIA.

I remember how annoyed my mother got. On a number of occasions I would be standing next to her, outside the car; we were tapping our feet, and my mother would cross her arms and heave a sigh, and my father would crook his finger at her, beckoning her over, as if he needed to ask her something. Eventually she'd lumber over, and he would pull her to his side and drape his arm around her shoulder, as if now she was doing something just as nice as the thing we were being held up from doing. He did this with all of us, with Casey and me. And I remember how cross I felt that day he took me and Pru to the Fillmore, at a gas station on Lombard, waiting for him to get off the phone, complaining bitterly to Pru, who said it didn't matter. He crooked his finger at me, beckoning me, and I shook my head and crossed my arms over my chest, and he kept crooking his finger, and I scowled and trudged over, calling for Pru to follow. I was sort of smiling when I got over to him, even though I was very annoyed, and he pulled me over to his side and draped his arm around me, and then reached over all the way to grab Pru by the nose.

"I worry about Pru," he said one day. We were walking along the path between the salt marsh and the bay. The tide was low, the marsh all muddy dunes, populated with sandpipers, killdeer, gulls, half a dozen kinds of ducks, and a swan. I remembered being on the Bolinas lagoon one morning at dawn with my father and brother. The sky was bright pale blue, marbled with gray and roses, and all of a sudden a whistling swan floated into view like magic, from around the bend, huge and white and perfectly silent. Casey took a picture of it, which he still had up on his wall, a not very clear photograph of the swan hidden partly by the bullrushes, in the sun-red lagoon at the base of the ridge. It was next to the picture he had of the young deer he nursed back to health at ten, lying in her nest of blankets out in our shed, the only two photographs on walls otherwise devoted to posters from the Fillmore Auditorium.

"Don't worry about Pru, Dad," I said.

"I know, but I do, anyway. Her mother's a real slob. And Pru's going to get into trouble. How does she do in school? Not so well, I would guess."

"Not so great. But it's mostly because the teachers don't like her."

"Casey's flunking English."

"He is?!" This was a first for our family, probably for the entire history of my family.

"He's stoned every weekend, we all know that. He comes home late Sunday, bleary-eyed, shot. I think they're doing acid in the hills. It does no good to ground him. All *hell* is breaking loose, baby doll." We tromped along. "This town is lost, that's for sure. I don't know. I don't know. If Casey survives these next few years, then you know what happens—he gets drafted and has to go to Vietnam. Or Canada. I feel like any way you cut it, we're going to lose him. I think this is why your mother's so depressed these days."

"She's always depressed about something."

"She's often depressed, not always. It's just unimaginably bad in the world right now. And we never seem to recover, it just gets worse. She keeps saying to her God, 'I don't get it; I don't get it,' and He doesn't say anything back. She keeps thinking He's going to pull a rabbit out of His hat. And yet of course she thinks He already has: the Lamb. And so she just grieves, because nothing makes sense to her anymore."

"Poor Mommy."

"What about me?"

"Poor Dad. Wanna get some french fries?"

"Sure I do. You buying?"

"I don't have any money." He smiled. We walked on, toward the waterfront dive at the end of the path.

"I'm sorry to be sounding so gloomy," he said.

"That's okay." He started to cough, and we stopped for a minute. I stared out to sea as he coughed.

"It's just that these really are difficult days. Too much happens in too short a time. Nothing sinks in. Half the time I feel made of rubber—but, at the same time, agitated, worried sick about your brother, always broke. I thought I'd be making more money by now. I thought I would have cut a wider swath."

I watched our feet as we walked along.

"None of the old rules hold up these days. None of them seem to apply. Even time, you know? You're too young to have studied this, but that's what Einstein proved—that clocks were a joke. They weren't measuring anything! They were chocolate bunnies!"

"You're ranting, Dad."

Neill Doughtery made the best french fries, like none I've had before or since. There was salt all over the plate when we finished. I took a sip of my father's cold beer, just to show him I was growing up. Sometimes to make this point to my parents, I would casually shoe-horn swear words into our conversations. "That damn wind!" I would say, or, unable to open a jar of jam, I would exclaim, "Oh, hell!" and they would smile nicely at me.

Out on the water in a space between two ratty boats, two brown ducks were paddling around on the silver green bay, floating, swimming back and forth. We could not see the shore from where we sat, because the wall below the windows blocked our view. My father raised his bottle of beer. "Here's to Pru," he said. "Here's to Casey." The ducks swam back and forth. Then they stood up, and looked for a moment as though they were dusting off their hands, after a job well done, and then they waded off, waddled away, purposeful and silly, out of our field of vision.

Natalie called to say she was almost certainly going to come up for my birthday, but wasn't sure who else would be along.

"If everyone's health holds," she added.

"Oh, that's fantastic," my mother said, but almost immediately went into a depression. She felt so lonely, it was almost too hard to have someone she loved so much come back into her life for a day or two, only to leave again. Also, we were being ostracized in town by the tennis club crowd, people with whom my mother had once been friends. It was all because of an article my father had written that month for the *Chronicle*. In it he had mentioned that the people of our town had a rate of alcoholism second only to the Indians in the Oakland ghettos. He mentioned the soaring divorce rate, the number of children on drugs, the general lab-rat confusion. "Why did the doctor's wife take another overdose?" he wrote. "Why do we drink as hard as the Indians do in Oakland?"

My brother's high school teacher xeroxed the article for all of his students, and Casey was a hero. The people who already loved my parents, the people in the McCarthy campaign, the people at my mother's church, were filled with praise for my father, and even Pru's slutty sister looked at me with new respect. But the tennis ladies punished us, passed us on the boardwalk and looked away, and their husbands gave us tight, bemused smiles.

There were couples I knew, the parents of friends, who fought so much that hell wouldn't have them, who were suddenly unified by their hatred of my father.

But my parents ended up fighting more. He was on a couple of talk shows, got a lot of attention, and acted different, loftier, and some of the most brilliant lines in the piece had been my mother's observations. One thing led to another, and they fought. They never fought in front of me and Casey, but I could always tell. I was still like a bat. The air in the room in which they had fought always felt different—thinner, charged, alive. Once not long before my birthday I walked into the living room on a dark rainy morning, and the white walls were dark gray, as dark as the sky outside, black gray. The windows beside the pane-glass door and the panes in the door themselves were rectangles of eerie jade green, the green of winter grass, and they were veined with the shadows of branches—and I somehow knew my parents had had a fight. They were not around, were not even in the house. Maybe in my sleep I had heard them hissing at each other, maybe not. Our windows were deep solid green and I knew that they had fought.

My mother was in a depression for a week after that. I couldn't stand being around her. She spent too much time talking to Jeffey. I thought she was crazy. Everything she did wore on my nerves. She turned on the gas burner before filling the tea kettle with water, as if you needed to let gas burners heat up, and I wanted to pick up the tea kettle and hurl it against the wall. She spread Marmite on her toast, which is a thick, almost black yeast spread the English are wild about. It looks like crankcase oil and it smells like the devil's toothpaste. A couple of times I brought Pru home after school and there she was, eating it, on toast, and I think I was more ashamed of her at those moments than Pru was about having a padlocked refrigerator.

But as with all of my mother's depressions, a day would come when I would walk into the kitchen and find her sitting somewhat dazed at the table, touching herself gingerly here and there, as if she had had a bad fall and was feeling around for broken bones.

"Hi," I said on the Sunday morning when she was pulling out of this latest slump.

"Hullo, lambie. Did you sleep?"

"Can I have some coffee today?"

"When did you start drinking coffee? All right, half a cup."

I got myself two-thirds of a mug of coffee, and doctored it with milk and sugar until it tasted like coffee ice cream.

"Where's the paper?" I asked.

"It didn't come today."

"God!"

"Darling, will you come to church with me?"

I protested at first, and then realized I had nothing to do, no paper to read, no homework, and Pru was grounded all weekend for getting a D in science. My mother got up and went into the Lion's Den, and after a minute I followed her there. She was sitting on the toilet, smoking dreamily, looking older. She had aged.

"Okay," I said, "I'll go."

We ended up walking there together. I wore fringe moccasins; she wore sky-blue heels. It was about a mile away, across the railroad yard, along the shore of the bay, through town. She was reasonably cheerful again, humming hymns.

"You think Natalie'll really come?"

"Yeah, I sort of think she will this time. I don't think she'll bring Lucy though."

"What about her and Uncle Ed?"

"What about them?"

I shrugged. "Never mind."

"Darling, it's okay to bring it up. It's just that I don't know the answers. I think they'll feel really strange around each other, but there'll be a lot of other people around."

"Yeah, like Peg."

"That's right. So it doesn't really make sense for the little girl to be in the middle of all that stuff, does it? I don't know how this will all shake down. God only knows."

"God is a cheese-dick," I said. I walked along staring at the ground. "I don't even believe in him anymore."

"Then how can He be a cheese-dick?"

"I don't know. What about Peg if Natalie comes?"

"Peg has been over and over and over all this in her head. She left Ed, and Ed and Natalie were lonely as a couple of clubfoots at the time, and one thing led to another. Now Natalie has a kid who looks like Lynnie. And everyone has paid through the nose. And amends have been made. Everyone's made sacrifices. So now this little kid is being raised by this nice new husband. She has two brothers who adore her. So, I don't know. Peg's okay with it now, I think. I mean, she's the lucky one, right? She ended up with Uncle Ed."

We had reached town. There were a lot more cars here now on a Sunday morning than there were two years ago. Plus several cute little breakfast cafes, several cute little stores that opened at ten on Sunday mornings. We didn't see anyone we knew.

"What about Lynnie?" I asked.

"Lynnie's so wrapped up in ballet."

"We never even have mentioned it for one second."

"Well, it was a pretty big deal. She took really nice care of Peg all along, even when things were at their worst; Peg lugging around that body bag of bad memories. But that was a long time ago. And Uncle Ed really loves her. So, we'll see."

It was great to be in church again. Everyone made a fuss over me. There were only three Anglos today, two at first, me and my mother, and then halfway through the first hymn, Wino John. I smelled his unmistakable smell and I felt my mother freeze up. Then he was pushing past me as though we were at a movie theater, and he pushed past my mother and sat down beside her.

She sighed and kept singing, O Freedom. After a moment, I could hardly smell the starchy smell of all that processed hair and all those burning candles—I could only smell John, grease, dirt, urine, port. He looked even worse than usual. His eyes were more bloodshot, and slightly yellow, ringed in red, half-open, full of pain; and the dirt was thicker and the hair more matted. I studied him while James read the opening prayer, "Do Thou meet us while we walk in the way, and long to reach the better country; so that following Thy light . . ." John wiped his snotty nose and mustache on the sleeve of his jacket. His beard and eyebrows were flecked with burrs and bits of grass. He began to scribble angrily on a scrap of paper, all the while hawking and sniffling away. I turned back toward the pulpit.

James said something that day that has stayed with me ever since. He said that on Christmas the year before, he and his wife had been driving across the bridge, to visit their children and grandchildren in San Francisco, and suddenly he had understood that the birds and the trees, the animals, the land, the flowers, the grasses, the fish and the whales, the sky and the water all knew that Christ was born; the Incarnation had happened, and everything knew, and the air shimmered with the knowledge of Christ's love and grace and reign.

And all the while the old man muttered, "Uh huh, oh yeah, aymen."

When we stood to sing another hymn, John remained seated, writing, hawking, but when we stayed on our feet after singing for the passing of the peace, he got up unsteadily.

At this church, beginning at one end of the rainbow-shaped rows of chairs, James hugged the first person and said, "May the peace of the Lord be with you." The person being hugged would reply "and with you," and then turn to the person on his or her left, hug that person and say, "May the peace of the Lord be with you." It was passed this way in the three semicircular rows until it got all the way over to the last person on the other end of the rainbow; much like "the wave" would later be done in ballparks, but slower. All of which meant that in several moments, my mother was to be hugged and passed the peace by John. I had seen him receive and pass the peace before, awkward, and of course no one wanted to linger in his arms for long, but people gave and received his hugs, whacking away for a second or two, turning then to hug the person to the left. But my mother had never been the one on his left. So I looked up at her and she bent down and whispered in my ear, "Pray for me."

I nodded, smiling.

The peace was getting closer.

"It won't be as bad as I'm imagining, will it?" my mother whispered to me. I shook my head, smiling.

Three people away, a mother hugged her tall chubby son, who turned to hug John, as my mother bent down to whisper, "I keep remembering Uncle Ed saying, 'Panic is your worst enemy,'" and I gave her the thumbs up sign, and she turned to be hugged by John.

She squared her shoulders and then raised her arms to encircle John's shoulders, but John squatted down, threw his arms around my mother's knees, and lifted her into the air.

I covered my mouth to stifle a scream. Her face was three feet above me, blank with fear and red with shame. He held her aloft, two feet off the ground, his horrible snotty face pressed against her stomach, and I thought that the eyes of the church were upon us, but no one, no one was watching. They were waiting for their hugs, or they had averted their eyes, and the disgrace in me was total. It was suddenly as if we, the three white people, were behaving in a scandalous way, here in the house of the Lord, while everyone passed the Peace of the Saviour, and it felt like an electrical storm was about to start. I reached up and grabbed a hunk of John's hair, and pulled, and saw that my mother was pinching him hard about the shoulders, trying to get her nails into his neck; he grimaced then, and put her down, rubbed his face on his sleeve, and yawned.

He stood there looking bored. My mother was trembling, rigid and shaking, and turned to me, full of fear and shame. I looked into her face, trying to seem kind, and she sat down and rubbed at her eyes. No one at all seemed to notice that anything strange had just happened. I turned to my left, and stood on my toes to give old Stephen a hug.

"Peace of the Lord be with you," I said.

"And with you."

Then I sat down and leaned against my mother, hard, and after a minute she put her arm around me, and her head against mine. She sighed again, and we stared at the stained-glass windows that hung suspended from the ceiling, wheat and grapes, bread and wine.

Later we walked home, and she said her heart felt broken, but she couldn't stand to talk about it yet. She said it had made her as afraid as she'd ever been before. She said she had felt abandoned by God, all alone in the world; until she had felt me leaning up against her. I didn't say anything. We sat down on a bench by the water so she could smoke. I wanted a cigarette so badly I could hardly stand it. White quilted clouds were reflected on the drab green water of the bay. There was a long cloud above San Francisco, with two parallel lines running its length and then disappearing into the bright blue sky, as if a skier had skied through it. Out on a piling streaked with tar, a pelican preened. My mother stared up into the sky as if she saw a plane approaching. There were thick ribbons of seaweed wrapped around all the driftwood on the beach. I had caught thousands of crabs on these shores. Now there would be new ones, all new crabs, under the rocks, under the logs. After a while my mother said, "Shall we?" and stepped back into her sky-blue heels, got to her feet, and headed home.

The following Sunday, one week before my birthday, I went to church again with my mother. I went as her bodyguard. This time we were the only two Anglos there. Everyone made a big fuss over me again. Wino John wasn't there. James pointed this out to the entire congregation, from the pulpit, as if my mother and I hadn't noticed.

"John is in the hospital," he said. "He is very sick. His liver is diseased. He is in trouble and really needs our prayers. I'm going up to see him after our service today, as he asked me to come and baptize him. Anyone here is invited to come along.

"I spoke to his sister in Minnesota last night. She said he has always had mental problems, since he was thirteen or so; he's schizophrenic, they say. Some of you have heard him play this here piano. He was classically trained. His sister said he was a child prodigy. I taped him once playing, if anyone here ever wants to listen. Once I was here an hour before the service, still working on my sermon, needing silence—this was maybe five years ago or so—and all of a sudden John showed up. He'd been to this church a few times before, but I hadn't ever spoken to him, and he asked me, 'Rev? Mind if I play around with your piano?' And he looked like we know him to look, maybe not so sick, a few years younger. His sister says he turned forty last year. And when he asked I thought, 'Heavenly Father, why do You do this to me?' But I told John to go ahead, and went back to my work, expecting to hear a commotion, like he was a kid who was going to pound on the keys—but I tell you, I heard the Holy Spirit playing through him. I heard God helping him play. He played quietly, hauntingly, like an angel, half-Mozart, half—wind chimes. So anyone here wants to go with me today, see me after the service."

My mother slowly bent her head back to stare at the ceiling of the quonset hut, and I knew then that we would be going.

We stood around his hospital bed, my mother and I, James, old Stephen, an aged black empress named Alice, and Alice's two teen-aged granddaughters. We were inside the curtains which separated him from the next bed. He looked better than he had in years, not so bleary, clean and shaved. His face and eyes were not so red, both were a little yellow. He wore a light blue paisley hospital gown, and there was a pleasantly skunky odor about him, like puppy breath. We all touched him. He looked sheepish, tired.

He looked out of the corner of his eyes, slyly. "Hey, Nanny," he said.

James filled a styrofoam cup with water, set it on the hospital table, and helped John get out of bed. His arms were as thin as a five-year-old child's. He stood with his back to the bed, his hair long and tangled, looking at his clean bare feet, at James' face, at mine, responding "I do" as James performed the sacrament. "Defend, oh Lord, this child with Thy Heavenly Grace," he read, and dipped the fingertips of his huge cupped hand into the styrofoam cup. He let his hand partly fill up with water and daubed it all over John's forehead.

It trickled down John's face, past his eyes, and James rubbed it into his cheeks, then caressed it into his neck.

John died three days later in his sleep, at the hospital. There was a service at our church and most of the congregation was there. My father and brother had come. The choir sang "Rock of Ages," "Beulah Land," the old man in the corner saying, "Uh huh, ay-men." James played the tape he had made of John playing piano. It was unlike anything I had ever heard in my life. The last notes hung in the air, some high like chimes, some like smoke. Everyone was crying, even my mother. James said that the music was God using John as an instrument, God playing John. The choir sang, "When I go up to Heaven I'll walk about, There's nobody there to turn me out; Deep River, my home is over Jordan." In a way I've never quite understood, the veil tore an inch for me that day, like it does every so often, when in the midst of all that is mundane and day-to-day, there's suddenly a tiny tear in the veil, and you see the bigger brighter thing, and then the veil repairs itself, and the day goes on as before.

A few days later, the last train left town for good. No one seemed to know that it was a historic day, that no train would run here again. This one train had been coming and going for nearly a month, and then one day it pulled out of town and didn't come back. There was no ceremony, no crowd, no nothing—but I was there. It was the day before my birthday, and I was walking into town, and this same diesel locomotive pulling one empty freight train slowly started up. The tracks were overgrown with brown grass and green weeds. The train briefly flattened the grasses like a hand running through a brushcut, the conductor blew the whistle, and that was that. Uncle Ed told us the next day that it wouldn't be coming back.

I was walking along the bay, by the railroad yard, and watched the train disappear around a bend. It was a foggy white day, and I was headed to Pru's. In the distance coming toward me from the direction of town, I saw a figure approach—a funny gypsy figure in ragged jeans like Wino John, long brown hair, my father's old Brooks Brothers vest. It was Casey. I waved to him. He walked toward me, but he didn't wave back, and I worried that maybe he would pass me by without saying hello. I felt a wave of loss in my stomach, my breathing grew rapid.

"Hey," I said when we got close.

"Hey," he said and stopped. He fished around in the pocket of his jeans. "Close your eyes," he said. He had something in his hand. I closed my eyes. "Stick out your hand." I had another wave of fear. I had spent my early childhood doing this, over and over ending up holding horrible and sometimes living things. I felt him put his fist on top of my palm and hold it there a minute. Then something slithered from his hand to mine, like a stream of sand. I opened my eyes, expecting the worst, but there in my palm was a thin silver chain, which held a crescent moon made of turquoise set in silver.

I gaped. He pawed the earth softly with one foot, trying to look cool. "Don't tell Mom and Dad," he said.

"Oh my God," I kept saying. I could have almost—out of joyful confusion—turned and flung it into the sea. I stood pouring the necklace slowly from one cupped palm to the other, the way we used to pass small heavy puddles of mercury from broken thermometers back and forth, from hand to hand when we were young. He was staring straight up, as overhead against the pure white, fog-white sky an egret glided past. "Look at that," he said. Then we stood there a minute not knowing what to say to each other, Casey acting bored, my own heart racing with relief and temporarily requited love.

"I gotta split," he said, and turned and walked away. There was a good-sized hole in the seat of his faded jeans. You could see a patch of pale skin. He didn't turn around to wave, and after a while he crossed the street and cut across the deserted railroad yard.

Natalie came up for my birthday after all, by herself. She flew up in the late afternoon of the big day, and was scheduled to leave at noon the following day. My mother and I picked her up in the Volkswagen bus. They couldn't take their eyes off one another, reaching out to touch each other's face, like blind lovers. Then Natalie started kissing me, taking my hand as we walked out the building, petting my stiffly set hair.

"You're almost as tall as me, Nanny girl. I love your hair that way. It was pretty the other way too," she said, which no one in my life ever had, ever, ever. "But this way, it's more you. Champagne blond. Lucky girl." I smiled and let go of her hand and walked on ahead. There was a huge burning rock in my throat. The two women limped along behind me. I thought about the day Natalie had moved away; about Wino John, and Casey, and I cried, wiping at tears, scuttling along like India Schuyler.

I raced to the car and stood there staring in as if there were someone inside I needed to talk to, smiling idiotically as my mother and Natalie approached, both of them looking quizzically at me.

While we were crossing the Golden Gate Bridge, Natalie said to my mother, "You look exactly the same."

"Oh, but I don't," said my mother. "I look in the mirror and say to myself, 'Where did you get that mask?' Inside I'm Nanny's age. Robbie has a friend named Gil, who turned seventy a month or so ago, and Robbie asked him what that feels like. And he said, 'I don't at all feel like a seventy-year-old. I feel like a young man who has something wrong with him.' "

I stared out at Alcatraz, and thought briefly about jumping off the bridge. "How come you have to leave tomorrow?" I asked.

"Matt's company dinner is tomorrow. I have to put on my rhinestones and slapshoes and dazzle the boss."

"Do you think you'll ever move back?"

"I don't know. I hope so. Matt's company may open an office up here next year. Then again they may not. It's all in the planning stages. We'll just have to play it all by ear. So who all's coming tonight?"

"Well, Ed and Peg," said my mother, "which you knew. And maybe Lynnie, but probably not. Casey. Sam and Bea Gold."

"How did their kid turn out?"

"Not so good. He's all caught up in this hippie shit, long hair, living in the Haight. Big drugs."

"Oh, God. What a funny little kid he was."

"Yeah. And Nanny's best friend Pru'll be there too."

"Whatever happened to Mady White?"

"It's kind of a long story," I said.

"Grandma Bette took her and Nanny to see *Whatever Happened to Baby Jane?*"

"Why on earth . . ."

"She thought it was about dolls."

"Oh. So what happened?"

"Mady freaked out," I said. "She threw up all over the place."

"What a toad. Does Robbie look the same?"

"Exactly. Maybe a little grayer around the temples."

Our house looked exactly the same, too, but with a lot more books in the living room, a couple of new paintings by an old friend named Stiek, more-recent pictures of us on the piano, and all new daddy longlegs in the corners.

I sat outside with my father and Natalie while my mother insisted on being alone in the kitchen. They talked about the war, about Ronnie the Rat and LBJ, about Casey and the twins.

"I pray now that the boys break their legs badly, lose their sight, or fingers. Anything."

"So do we, darling."

"You don't pray, though, Robbie."

"On this one thing I do."

"Does Casey have a girl?"

"Casey has a secret life. He could be married and have children for all we know."

"Robbie? Is this going to work out okay?"

"Being with Ed and Peg, you mean? Yes, I think it will."

And it did, at least in my eyes. Everyone seemed perfectly at ease, although maybe a little shy. The evening passed in a flash. I don't remember anyone seeming edgy or angry or sad. It was just some run-of-the-mill family party, no big deal, lots of food and music and laughter. My father's version was somewhat different:

"I would say it was the longest three hours of my life. Right there, baby, is all you need to know—what other party in our entire history lasted only three hours? Your mother was a wreck. If you had walked up behind her in the kitchen and tapped her on the shoulder, she would have screamed bloody murder. Peg as it was bit a hole in her own tongue, while having a nice little talk with Natalie about the weather. She spent half an hour in the bathroom spitting out blood, running cold water over her tongue. Ed was as close to drinking as he's been since he quit—he told me later that the jungle drums were beating all night, and a still, small voice inside him said that *maybe* his problem all along had only been that he drank too *fast*, you see. He said he felt like there was a knife twisting in his guts. Sam sat there looking like he was waiting to see his proctologist. Natalie was a hero, though. Of course she and your mother both had quite a lot to drink. And Casey was so stoned, I seriously doubt he has any memories of the evening at all."

But he did: "It was like everything that's wrong with this country," his version began. "Everyone caught up in the lie, that everything is okay. Everyone just trying to be clever and to look like they've got their act together. All this time just *passing*, being killed. All this incredibly heavy shit is hitting the fan in this country, all around the world, and everyone sits around saying, 'Isn't this just the most marvelous cheese?' Dad going around whacking everyone on the shoulders, all very jovial and good old boy, spouting all his great bleeding-heart liberal theories, telling jokes he'd told a hundred times before."

Years later I asked my mother, "What do you remember of that night?"

She said, "I remember how kind and heroic your father was, how calm and generous, taking on all that tension himself, dancing as fast as he could to keep the conversation going, to help people stay reasonably comfortable. Casey was really high; your father didn't want to deal with him at all, but he didn't lay some heavy trip on him. He tried to let it go. I prayed the entire evening, but still, God, it was hard. But it didn't have to be perfect, and it meant that down the road Peg and Natalie could work things out in a way that was more real. You know—more authentic. Ed did great, I thought. I think his heart really ached, wanting to talk to Natalie, wanting to ask about Lucy. Natalie had known that it wouldn't be a piece of cake, and it wasn't. It was hard on everyone. But it was sort of beautiful, too, in its own way."

It hadn't been hard on me at all, maybe because my father was letting me and Pru and Casey drink a little beer. Normally, then as now, if everyone around me is comfortable, I can relax and be comfortable too, and if everyone—no, if *anyone* is nervous, I sit there psychically panting like an old woodchuck. But the night of my twelfth birthday, I was blessedly blind and oblivious, wearing the necklace my brother had stolen, hidden under a rose-colored poorboy Pru's sister had given to me.

Ed and Peg arrived at the same time as Sam and Bea, and suddenly the house was filled with adults, everyone but Ed drinking old man diGrazia's latest batch of dago red, old man diGrazia now in his eightieth year. Joan Baez was on the stereo, and Peg and Natalie gave each other a little hug when they first saw each other, as did Ed and Natalie—an even shorter hug, and everyone was talking at once, except for Peg, who had gone into the bathroom. I suppose, looking back, that this was when she had bitten through her tongue. When she finally got out, she took a seat by Sam Gold. I went over to see her.

She pulled me in against her, so that I was sort of leaning into her lap, actually sitting on one of her thighs, and she buried her face in my back, and we sat like that for a while. I didn't particularly notice she was feeling pain. In fact, it didn't even cross my mind. And I sat on her, listening to Joan Baez until, over all the commotion, I heard Pru scratching at the door like a dog.

Something bad had happened to Pru the weekend before. A boy gave her hickeys, on her breasts. He was a friend of her sister's, three years older than Pru, whom Alison's boyfriend had brought over when he came to see Alison. Pru told me several days later, while we lay by the creek that ran beside what had been the rec center. "We had all this rum and Coke," she said. "And then Allie put on some records and we danced. Then she and her boyfriend went to her room, and this boy and I had more to drink, and a bunch of cigarettes, and we were just sitting on the couch, talking, and then we started making out. It was really nice. Then he started feeling me up, and then he pulled my bra down, so it was around my waist, and then he was kissing my boobs, and then he was giving them monkeybites." She was flushed, squinting up at the sun. There were blackberry bushes behind her, water skeeters all over the creek, guppies and tadpoles floating by in schools. There were no berries on the blackberry bushes. We could hear the thwock-thwock-thwock of tennis balls in the background, the piping and cries of children in the pool, cars, and unseen birds like fingerbells. "And he just kept doing it, giving them hickeys. It sort of hurt a little, I don't know." I felt the tightening down there in my crotch. Her roots were growing out again. I was scared and jealous, as flushed as Pru.

I opened the door and stepped outside. She had toned down the ratted hair and Nefertiti eyes for the evening. "Let's go have a smoke," I whispered. We went under the house, and sat in the little space next to the water heater, surrounded by pipes, a ladder, old half-gallon cans of turpentine and linseed oil, the black cat carrier, filmy curtains of cobwebs.

She fished around in her purse and pulled out a can of beer, which she opened and handed to me. I took a long sip, as if I were desperately thirsty. She got out her white lipstick and we both put some on, and then she fished around some more and got out her Marlboros and some matches. She shook one out for each of us, lit her own and then mine. I touched her hand as if to steady it as she held the match to my cigarette, like a woman in the movies. We heard a car door open and Casey say something and slam the door, and we heard the car pull away, then Casey's footsteps on the dirt walkway leading to the front door. We sat smoking in silence. She went back into her purse and pulled out a wrapped present, with a ribbon just like the one on Peg's present to me—paper grosgrain curled with the edge of the scissors into tight ringlets of ribbon. It was bikini underpants, a white lacy pair, a black lacy pair.

"Oh, my god, I can't believe it," I said, several times. We finished up the beer, then stubbed out our cigarettes, and I had Pru put the underpants back in her purse, so I could smuggle them into my room later. We heard my mother open the back door and call my name. I bellowed that I would be right there.

"Right now," my mother yelled.

"God!" I said to Pru, letting my shoulders drop two inches, as if my mother wanted me to come in and scrub the kitchen floor. "I guess we better go in."

"This oughta be good," she said. It was Pru's first adult dinner party, as her mother never, ever, had company over, except for the occasional boyfriend. Pru's mother went out most evenings. Joan Baez had been replaced with The Weavers, and my father was letting the three of us kids drink beer. My mother had made roast beef and Yorkshire pudding, and all the adults except Ed drank lots of wine and laughed and talked and were nice to Pru, especially Natalie, and all in all for Pru, compared to her own strange cold household, the evening was lively and loving.

After dinner we all moved back into the living room, to wait for my mother to dish up the cake. I was a little bit drunk. Pru and I were sharing the piano bench, and Ed had gone to sit next to Natalie for a few minutes. Then he got up and hurried after Peg, who had dashed to the kitchen. After a minute the lights in the living room went out, and Peg carried in the cake, her face illuminated by the thirteen candles, one to grow on. My mother walked in behind her, carrying a stack of plates, with Ed beside her, carrying a knife and some napkins. Everyone clustered around me and Pru at the piano, everyone craning forward to see how my mother had decorated the cake. Ed tried to shoo people away with waves of his hand, as if they were all rubbernecking at the scene of a car accident. "Hey, come on, come on," he said, "haven't you people ever seen a cake before?" and it made Peg giggle so hard that she had to stand there in front of me holding the cake with her legs crossed.

I made a wish and blew the candles out. I don't remember what I wished for, probably a boyfriend, or breasts. Some time later, after coffee and cake, after I opened my presents while listening to Woody Guthrie, everyone started to leave. After helping with the dishes Ed and Peg drove Pru home. My father slept in my bed, and I slept with my mother and Natalie in my parents' bed. Natalie was in the middle. I slept with my arm draped around her. She smelled of lemons, soap, and wine. I passed out early on; but they were awake until dawn. Every time I woke up, they were still talking softly in the dark.

||| FOR NEARLY a year now I have
been living back in the town where I grew up, in an illegal mother-
in-law unit half a mile away from my mother. She would be old
enough to retire now, if she had a job. She works, but not for money,
serving at soup kitchens, visiting hospitals, registering voters. My
brother lives across the bay in San Francisco, half a block away from
his ex-wife and their nine-year-old son Rob.

He was in town a few days ago for the wedding of his old friend
Owen Turner, Mighty Owen Turner, who now works for the Bank of
America, votes Republican, and wears a beige hairpiece to match
what is left of his thinning beige hair. Casey was one of the ushers.
He wore a rented tuxedo, cropped his beard for the occasion, and
picked us up an hour before the ceremony was to begin. We drove
into town for gas before heading up the hill to the little white
church. The town is not the same place where we grew up. It is like
a game of Monopoly now. The entire length and width of the railroad yard is filled with a dense development of condominiums and
office buildings and restaurants. The view to the left as you drive into
town from my mother's house—of the wild blue scintillant bay, An-

gel Island, Alcatraz, the Golden Gate Bridge, the city—is still so beautiful it can make you feel almost desperate; but below the view, between the road and the shore is a series of rolling grassy knolls, low and perfectly manicured. It looks like you are at a golf course or a retirement community for the rich. It looks like a town where children are not allowed.

At the gas station my brother told the attendant to fill it up, and the three of us climbed out of the car. Casey usually pumps the gas himself, but he didn't want to get gas on his tuxedo. My mother and I went into the ladies' room, and Casey went to use the pay phone, to check in with the foreman at the house he was remodeling. When my mother and I came out of the bathroom, Casey was still on the phone. My mother and I stared at each other. Casey glanced over, and crooked his finger at us, beckoning. We both shook our heads. He did it again and again, crooking his finger. I stared down at the ground, sort of smiling, and then walked over to him. He reached out to pull me in closer and then draped his arm around me. We stood there for a few more minutes while he talked.

My mother stood nearby smoking, staring up at the little white church on the hill. It was surrounded by tiny cars and figures. My mother was sixty-three this year. She looks somewhat older than that. Thin people as a rule age more dramatically. Her hair turned white when my father got sick. It is shoulder length but she always wears it up, loosely. Her skin is fair but she looks like someone who has been smoking her whole life. We see each other nearly once a week for a meal or a movie. She is very careful not to wear out her welcome, although of course it is I who have moved back to town. We are pretty close, although she still says things that make my stomach or hands clench up, that make me go from being the daughter of the year to a person who would like to smash her in the face and break her nose. She asks me if I have met any interesting men and I want to scream. I have asked her maybe two hundred times not to ask me this one question, but every few weeks she asks again. She used to do this to me in seventh and eighth grade, when Pru and I went to dances in our minis and our poorboys, our black fishnet stockings, white lipstick, fringe moccasins. I would come home having eaten a package of Certs on the way, to cover up the beer and cigarettes on my breath, and she would ask me nicely if anyone had asked me to dance. And I would look at her like she had cat shit on her clothes.

Now she calls and before saying hello, blurts out things like, "Darling, let me put the ice cream away!" and I protest, "Mom, *you* called *me*," but at least now she doesn't call me first thing in the morning. The first morning that I was back, she called me at seven-fifteen.

"Hello, darling," she said. "How was your first night home?"

"Mom, you don't call people at 7 a.m.!"

"But darling, I thought you got up early. I mean, you tell people you do."

"What, are you saying now I lie?"

"Oh, honey."

"Do you call Natalie at seven?"

"Sure, sometimes."

"Well, don't call me till nine. I don't want to talk until then."

So the next morning the phone rang at a quarter to ten, and when I picked it up, she said urgently, "Did I wake you?"

My brother and mother and I drove past the private club where the rec center used to be. The hills above it were covered with condominiums. These were the hills, once shaggy and bare, where walking at dusk with my father one night, we came upon a gypsy camp. The gypsies gave my father a glass of red wine in a red coffee cup. There were buildings being built on these hills by the time I turned twelve. Pru and I used to come sit in the empty frames on the weekends, smoke cigarettes and dope, discussing what we would do with our lives, listening to rock and roll on Pru's transistor radio.

Pru got killed in Santa Cruz when she was twenty-one; in the mountains; raped and strangled. We hadn't been friends for years, but I couldn't stop crying when my mother told me the news. My mother was crying, too. After eighth grade when I went off to a little hippie high school in San Francisco, Pru stayed and went to the local public high school, although daily attendance was not her strong suit. I'm sure she just barely, barely got by. I would see her over the years, and we would both be somewhat embarrassed, I in my best hippie Indian clothes, she in minis and dominatrix boots, me with no makeup, Pru all dolled up like a hooker. I cried one day when we ended up at a bus stop together, and she shared a half-pint of warm vodka with me. I cried after she got on her bus and I started to think of what a great friend she had been, of what a stroke of luck it had been to find her coming out of the record store that day, of how when I came to that place on the tracks God or life threw the switch, and I ended up with Pru, and with all that that meant: it meant I belonged. She was thinner that day at the bus stop. She had probably discovered speed. We were fifteen years old. After she died, her mother sold the laundromat. It has been replaced by a fancy chocolate store.

I saw Pru's mother in downtown San Francisco a few years ago, near Union Square. She didn't look nearly as old as my mother, although she is in fact three years older. Her hair was still black, although I'm sure she dyed it, and her face and eyes must have been done a number of times: she definitely had that look of surprise and innocence, like we used to see at the rec center when women would wear swim caps that were too small for them. She was emaciated and dressed very stylishly, in a short denim dress, with black stockings and black heels.

She was at the intersection, waiting for the light to change.

I almost ducked back and waited for her to cross the street, but I wanted to tell her what a huge difference Pru had made in my life. I tapped her on the shoulder, and when she turned around, I felt just like I had every time she opened the door to me when I was young—afraid and obsequious.

"Hello, Mrs. Wallace," I said.

She looked at me intently. "Hey there," she said, and looked back at the light to see if it had changed. Then she smiled a little and began to fish around in her purse. She found her cigarettes, shook one out, offered the pack to me, and when I declined, lit her own. It was as long as a pencil.

"Are you living in the city?" I asked.

"Yeah. Not so far from here."

"Where is Alison?"

"Down in Ojai, married to a dentist. They have three little kids. Not so little anymore." She turned to watch the light. It didn't change. She wasn't going to say anything else to me.

"Well," I said. I could hear the clank and purr of a backhoe somewhere nearby, tearing up a city street, the flutter and cries of the pigeons at Union Square above the scraping and rumbling and hum. I stood there behind Mrs. Wallace like a jerk for a minute, trying to think of something to say, but then the light changed and she turned to say good-bye.

"Nice to see you," she said.

"You, too." She stepped off the curb, and I stood where I was and watched her go. Her steps were small and precise, due perhaps to the tight skirt and high heels; in any case, while everyone else in the crowd strode or bustled or lumped across the street, she looked as if she were trying to walk a perfectly straight and important line, a field sobriety test or a tightrope wire.

Casey was looking at me in his rear-view mirror.

"What."

"You look pretty."

"No, I don't."

"Now you stop that, girl. Or me and your mother'll take you straight back to the home. Won't we, Ma?"

My mother nodded, turned to my brother, and smiled. This is always the family threat, that we'll put one another back in the home, where we won't like it at all because they always take our things.

"And you don't like it there at all," he said. "And do you remember why?"

"Because they always take my things."

"That's right."

"Ed says he needs you to call him," I said.

"When did you see him?"

"Yesterday."

"Okay." From up here all the buildings in the railroad yard, the restaurants and shops with their blue awnings and the condos and the little bridge and the little lake look like a scale model an architect has built, peopled with half-inch plastic people, plastic dogs, and plastic trees. "Dear God," my father used to say.

"What did Ed have to say?" my brother asked.

"Mostly we talked about Dad."

Yesterday Ed was waiting for me in a booth at Nellie's coffee shop. He had just run out of coffee when I walked in, and he was holding up his cup, crying "Nurse! Nurse!" It was hard to see him sometimes because he looked so much like my father, and it was hard to think of Lynnie still getting to have him, to have a father, and how her kids would get to grow up around him—crazy old beautiful Ed.

"I don't think we'll ever get used to it," he said to me halfway through our breakfast. "I feel him around me sometimes though. And you know I don't have no truck with real religion, with all that 'who shot the Holy Ghost' crap. But several times when I've been really low, late at night, before the dawn, or hell, who knows, midday, I've suddenly been aware of your Dad, crouched on the floor in the corner, sort of like a bird, just waiting there for me, keeping me company. Several times I've felt him sitting on my side of the bed, like I was a kid with a fever. Your mother says she feels this about Jesus sometimes—I remember once she was trying to explain this to your Dad and me—this was a long time ago, because I was still drinking. We were all over at your place. Lucy had just been born."

"Lucy? You mean Lynnie."

Ed struck his forehead. "Lynnie," he said. "Your mother said she felt Jesus was like a scent in her life, in every room, and she also felt Him sort of following her around, moving around close by in whatever area she was in, like He was going back and forth around her, and your father said, 'Rather like a pool sweep, darling?'" Ed burst out laughing. I laughed too, and the waitress brought us more coffee. Nellie died the same year my father did.

"After Dad got sick, he sort of vaguely believed that Zen thing that if there was a God, it wasn't an old man, it was the spirit of a baby."

"He told me the same thing, too. It always struck me as funny—that he ended up with a bright hard-core leftie who actually believed in Jeeesus. He sure loved her, though. He sure loved your mother. Those first ten years or so, though, I swear, their marriage was a three-legged race through life."

"Wasn't yours and Peg's?"

"Yeah, probably. Of course it was, me drunk all the time."

"Sometimes I feel like I don't really care what happens, since Dad is dead."

"That'll pass someday. We have to give it more time." He stared down into his coffee cup. "The other day I realized how it feels to me. It's like when Peg and I had that view of the harbor, the mountain, the sky, that fabulous grove of pear trees down below us, between us and the railroad yard. But then Archer built that goddamn condominium there, and Peg and I would stare out the window—where we'd always stood to watch the pear trees, leafless or budding or drooping with pears—and our hearts would just sink. Just fucking sink. Because—you know the pear trees are still there, but you can't see them anymore.

"You keep looking out the window, and each time you're reminded of what was once there, and how much pleasure it brought you, and you gamely say to yourself that it's still an exquisite view, that you can still see the mountain, some of the bay, Angel Island, Alcatraz, the sky, and a million birds, but the goddamn pear trees are gone."

You can just see the top of the mountain from the steps of the little white church, so dark green as to almost look black. Casey went around in back to be with the other ushers, and my mother and I went inside briefly to lay our sweaters down on a pew in this plainest of all churches. Then we went outside, said hello to the other early arrivals, and went to stand by ourselves on the wide cracked steps that lead partly down the hillside. We sat down so my mother could smoke in comfort. The view was fantastic to the south, toward San Francisco: of the bay, the Golden Gate Bridge, the islands. The steps were badly cracked and beautiful, eight feet wide, speckled with rust orange moss, surrounded on three sides by fabulous tall windswept golden grass. I felt like having a cigarette, but did not want to start smoking again. One puff and I'd be on my third pack by midnight. In the spring the grass up here is brilliantly, crazily green, and a million wildflowers bloom, poppies and leopard lilies, monkey flowers, buttercups, and the dark garnet-red black jewel flowers. I brought Ed's daughter Lucy up here once, to see them. My father had been dead about a year, and Lucy had just started studying art at San Francisco State. She was very shy and quiet, like Lynnie, but prettier. She grew up knowing that Ed was her biological father, and called him Ed on the rare occasions she came to town with Natalie.

Her real father was Natalie's husband Matt. He had been transferred to San Jose ten years ago, so my mother and Natalie got to see each other every few months. Lucy and Ed were friendly in a very sad and shy way with each other. She no longer wore horn-rims or even glasses but contact lenses that made her eyes crazy jewel blue, and she looked at Ed shyly with blue laser eyes.

My mother smelled of smoke and Chanel No. 5. We were sitting quite close together on the steps. There were almost no wildflowers this time of year, in all of that windswept gold grass, but near the steps and growing out of the cracks were stalks of yarrow, that white and feathery fern, as well as some poppies and patches of wild mint.

The church bells were ringing. When we turned around, a lot of people had arrived, were standing around outside or filing in, the women on the arms of ushers.

"Pru and I used to come up here a lot," I said.

"I never knew what the two of you did."

"We'd sit here and smoke, talk about things. Sometimes we would make garlands for our hair." I saw us then, twelve and thirteen, me all skin and bones with white processed hair, Pru still with her baby fat, sitting up here, staring off to sea. Pru had had an abortion. She had let a boy have sex with her, a friend of her sister's, a sixteen-year-old boy. She had to stay overnight at a hospital in the city. Her mother had beaten her black-and-blue. Pru, who had had to tell the doctor that she was raped, also told him that the man had given her the bruises. Her sister stayed with her at the hospital. The doctor helped her set up a cot next to Pru's bed. We didn't talk about it very much but I stopped smoking dope for a while because it was so scary to think about stoned: the sex and the abortion.

My mother got to her feet and offered me her hand. I shook my head. "I want to stay here a few more minutes," I said and she nodded. I watched her walk up the steps in her dressy white sandals; she doesn't wear high heels anymore. There were several dozen people in front of the church, its white A-frame against the truest blue sky, on the hill in a field of prairie gold grass. Up in front of the church were people Casey and I went to school with, some of them with their children and babies and parents. I saw five older couples, my mother's friends, standing together, all of whom I had known my whole life. Some had worked with my mother for McCarthy or McGovern or Carter, some were Republicans, but they had all been friends forever, and they had all lost a child in the sixties and early seventies. All of them had other children too, thank God, some of them ushers and bridesmaids today, and all of them were handsome and fit but made old by loss. Ginny Cohen died in Juvenile Hall of a drug overdose when she was fifteen. Doyle Yeats drowned in the lagoon, drunk, the same year. Eleanor Hunter died mysteriously in Peru when she was eighteen. Mattie Gold died in a backpacking accident, high on LSD. Ben Atchison died in a car crash with four other kids. There were probably a lot of other parents here today whose children had died, but they were not so noticeable, not all standing together. Everyone seemed happy. It was a wedding, after all. I was incredibly depressed.

I kept thinking of my own wedding—not in a church but in our ramshackle house just across the street from the Petaluma River, across the road from the low hills, bright green in the spring, shaggy and golden in summer. And of how the morning after our wedding, we awoke as the sunrise was opening up like a flower behind and below one of these hills, coloring the river rose and orange, so desperately full of love for each other we could hardly contain ourselves. "Please," he said smiling, studying my face as if the meaning of life were on it, "let me go out and kill somebody for you."

It was nuts to have married him. There were any number of reasons why I did. One was that he didn't want to make love all that often, and neither did I at the time. It didn't feel safe anymore. It brought up feelings in me of violation and foreboding, as if maybe something bad had happened to me as a child. It felt sometimes when I was in bed with a man that I was encouraging him to do whatever he wanted with me so that he would not fuck the three-year-old in the corner, so that he would not even notice her there. So it was convenient that he could go for days without wanting to make love. And also he was handsome and charming, and I thought that reflected well on me. When Lynnie and Peg first met him, I was already feeling that maybe he secretly wasn't a very good man, but when I half expressed my fears to them, Lynnie said, "Look, we don't care if he *beats* you."

"Why are you looking so sad?" my mother asked. She had returned from having mingled with the other guests, and sat beside me on the steps.

"I guess because it's a wedding. It makes me sad."

"Uh huh."

"And plus I miss Dad."

"Me too."

I hadn't been in a church since a month or so after my father died. My mother and I limped to her church one Sunday. The old man in the corner was still miraculously alive, almost a hundred, still in the corner, stooped and faded. There were mostly women, mostly older. The ones who were more or less my age still had processed hair. Singing, they looked so beautiful, so free. Their little girls had heads full of braids and bright plastic barrettes. This generation was growing up proud, you could see something close to sassy in their faces and in how secretly pleased they were when they got to nod or shake their heads, and their braids were tossed around and the bright little barrettes in the shapes of airplanes and stars and animals tapped lightly against each other. I closed my eyes.

James wasn't there anymore. There was a woman preaching, the

Reverend Ms. Jana Smythe, who read the passage in John where Jesus is being crucified, with his mother Mary and Magdalene and the wife of Cleophas all at the foot of the cross.

"The women were last at the cross and first at the tomb," someone once said."

And the old man in the corner said, "Ay-men."

"There as the Saviour was dying, one of the most painful deaths of all."

"My Lord."

"Forsaken, broken, His heart nearly broken with sorrow."

"Uh huh."

"And that is the human experience! But there at the foot of the cross, huddled together, alone—there were no crowds, no lines."

"No lines!"

"And He cried out to his mother, 'Woman, behold thy son!' And in that moment we see all of human pain and suffering; the hopelessness of human love, the helplessness of it all. 'Love dies,' the world says, 'just give it time,' but they stayed with this man. They stayed with him, huddled together, and that is maybe all we can do, and maybe it shows that life has more power than death, and maybe it shows that love has more power than hate." That was what it felt like when my father lay dying; like he was being crucified, and all we could do was sit with him huddled together.

"What are you thinking now?" my mother asked on the steps of the little white church.

"No lines!" I said, and she smiled.

Half of the people milling around outside the church or filing in were the grown-up children Casey and I had gone to school with. They all knew me during the years I straightened my hair. I was not eager to go up and make small talk and have them remember or say what I looked like in those days.

Pru had taken me into the city the first time so I could get my hair chemically straightened like black people do, but at a white beauty salon her sister knew about. I just wanted to look like everyone else. I just wanted to look like anyone else. To have long blond hair I could fling off my shoulders and then fling around until it fell over my face and breasts, and then to fling it back over my shoulders like a bridal bouquet. I did not have flingable hair, even after it was straightened. That was all I wanted out of life: the hair, the breasts, the boyfriend. I had to sleep with my hair in plastic curlers every night so that it would be straight in the morning. It was like sleeping on a pillow-case full of roller skates. I have a confusion of feelings when I think now of the little girls at my mother's church tossing their braids about, the braids secured and weighted down with bright barrettes.

"Let's go up, darling. Casey keeps giving us the eye."

"I just feel funny."

"I know."

"I'm the only one here without a husband."

"Well, what about me?"

I hung my head and nodded, then I looked over at her and smiled. "Will you wait here with me a few more minutes?"

"Uh huh."

The second time I had hypnosis, several weeks ago, I remembered all sorts of things I hadn't recalled the first time—lots of bad moments of romance, some with a man who was now up above us being an usher, a romance during which I generated enough pain for myself to keep Berkeley lit for a year. But mostly I saw a lot of childhood scenes that I may not have thought about since they happened, scenes of how frightened and ashamed I had been and of how little comfort there was. One scene involved a good half dozen of the grown-up children here at the wedding today. I was six years old, and my father and I were walking along the path by the salt marsh, and we came upon ten children from my first-grade class who were all celebrating Mady White's birthday. Somehow I had not been invited. They were all sitting within a ring of wild animals—egrets and herons mounted on driftwood, a snowy owl, a red-tailed deer, a raccoon, a silver fox. The children were seated on a plaid blanket surrounded by these animals, the girls in little dresses, the boys in slacks and blazers; and it was all like a dream, and I felt like howling with pain as I stood there hand in hand with my father, who then let go of my hand to reach for the pen and paper in his breast pocket. And the children cried hello to me and waved happily from inside the ring.

The thing was, I hadn't even cried. After I had played through all of my memories and come to the earliest one, at the hospital at three and a half years old, when I screamed in the middle of the night, the hypnotist asked if I had cried at the time. I shook my head. "I want you to try to find all the tears you didn't cry," he said. "Just stay with the feelings, and see where they take you."

They took me to a cathedral.

In the dream or whatever it was, I found myself on the lawn of a magnificent church, and knew that I was to walk inside, that someone was waiting for me.

It was a solemn and secret place. A high worship was going on. Everyone at the altar was in fabulous vestments, brightly colored, and mystical music was playing, Gregorian chants. But I went off to a small chapel to the left of the main nave, where inside the altar faced east. The room was lit by candles and the sun shone through stained-glass windows, and Gregorian chants were being sung in here also, quietly, deeply. All the people—all the players—of my life were here, the immediate family gathered around the altar, and on the altar there was a golden casket, like the ones in which they bury the relics of the saints. My first thought was that I had died and that everyone I'd ever known was here to bury me. Pru was alive again, as was my Grandmother Bette, as was my father. The pressure and weight on my chest after I saw my father made it hard to breathe and the air was too thin. Then I took my place at the head of the coffin.

Someone opened it slowly and a baby was brought out, a baby girl still alive, and I knew who it was. She was handed to me. I was amazed, just amazed. I looked at the face of the bright docile baby I was holding and saw the movie of what her future had been—in schoolyards and classrooms, in the branches of trees, at holiday dinners, at dances, in beauty salons, in rivers, at concerts, on mountains, on drugs, in bars and beds and churches. Here she was, just looking around, just taking it in; and I believed right then that I was being given back what I had been born with; or that at least it was still alive.

On the steps of the little white church my mother was rubbing my shoulder. "Casey's snapping his fingers at us," she said. There was a small white cloud on the very top of the mountain. The church bells had stopped ringing. My mother looked very pretty. Her hair was up somewhat more formally than usual, and she was wearing an evergreen silk dress my brother bought her last year for Lynnie's wedding. I had made her put a little blusher on her cheeks. She leaned over to kiss me behind one of my ears and stayed that way, nuzzling me. She was wearing Peg's gorgeous fake pearls, and I could feel them on my skin. Her breath was warm and sweet and a little smokey. She was breathing through her nose. I used to wonder if more air went in and out of her big nostril than in and out of the other. I sighed and looked down at my feet: I was wearing my mother's old sky-blue heels. Pru taught me to walk in heels. She was as pigeon-toed as a shy person, even—or especially—when we were sitting down. Here on the steps the day Pru told me about her abortion, she was wearing green suede ankle-length boots, pointy and stolen, and black fishnet stockings. We wove garlands of tiny daisies for our hair, frail wreaths, one for my white-blond black-people's hair, one for her bleached and straggly mane with its cap of mink-brown roots: we just sat there on the steps of the church for a while, looking out, looking down. My mother got to her feet and then offered me her hand. "We'd better go," she said. "Now he's tapping the face of his watch." I looked over my shoulder at Casey, who was signaling us with extreme agitation. I smiled up at my mother and she smiled at me. She could see that I was more or less okay. I held up my hand and she grasped it, and as she pulled me to my feet I stared down at the sky-blue heels of hers I was wearing, at the orange moss on the cracked concrete steps, at the poppies and the sprigs of wild mint.